THE UNSPOKEN TRUTH
AND
LIFE STORY

KEENAN HUDSON

Blue Heron Book Works, LLC

Allentown, Pennsylvania

Copyright © 2022 Keenan Hudson

All rights reserved.

ISBN: 978-8-9871459-0-6
All images property of the author
Cover design: Solasta Digital
Cover photo: Lydiana Gonzalez
www.keenanhudson.com
www.blueheronbookworks.com

DEDICATION

I would like to dedicate this book to my Mother Bernetta "Tina" Hudson and Grandmother Nancy "Mom-Mom" McBride who are both in a better place. These two were the epitome of Great People. Had not their teachings, moral standard, and well-rounded principles been instilled in me as a child I would not have been able to write this book. Without a shadow of a doubt, they are proud of the chains that were broken and goals that I've accomplished.

Contents

ACKNOWLEDGMENTS i

INTRODUCTION 1

Growing up 3

Alone in The House After My Mother Passed 14

Photo Album of My Family 20

How It Went Down 26

My Lawyer 30

My Arrest 33

Who Ratted on Who 43

Culture Shock 48

Becoming a Man in Prison 57

The Business of Education and Business 63

Learning Music and Finding God 66

A Parole Plan in Hand 79

....To Here 87

Photo from now 89

APPENDIX 90

ENDORSEMENTS OF KEENAN HUDSON 115

CONNECT WITH KEENAN 119

ACKNOWLEDGMENTS

First, I would like to give all the Glory and Honor to the strength of my Life which is God Almighty from whom all Blessings flow. Without him, I am nothing. With him, I live, move, and have my being.

Second, I want to thank Mrs. Sonia Jennings and Mr. Ted Jennings for being the reason of me developing my faith in God.

Third, I want to thank Ms. Donna who walked with me through every step of my return to normal life, from teaching me how to open a bank account, learn how to drive, and master the credit game. Also, Pastor Alex and Amelia Velazquez (RIP) for laying out a re-entry strategy platform for me that had a positive impact on my transitioning.

Fourth, I want to thank my publisher, Blue Heron Book Works, for their diligent help in writing the narrative of where I come from, who I am, and where I'm headed.

Fifth, I want to thank my marketing team, Solasta Digital, for utilizing the proper tools and arranging for this book to be a success.

And last but not least, I am so appreciative of all family, friends, and other supporters who believed in me and believe that this book will be a great success.

Thank You and Much Love To All Of You.

INTRODUCTION

In 1989 I felt like my life was in danger. I opened my eyes and I saw nothing but strangers.

That day was my birthday, that is, the day I was born. My mom was there, of course. My dad too. My grandma, uncles, aunts. My older brother was around somewhere, but we gave each other wide berth ever since I can remember until I was released from prison 30 year later, so I wasn't aware of his presence. But I was aware that the room was full of people, people who said they loved me, and I believe that they did. But any hopes and dreams they had for me, were drowned out by the reality that a poor kid born in a poor section of Philadelphia was already just a player in someone else's play, a play in which my part routinely ended in incarceration or early death.

It would take me more than 30 years to write my own story, and I'm writing this book to tell you who Keenan Hudson is, what my story is. To tell you about the things I've been through and how I overcame the obstacles in my path to become the person I am now, the person I am still trying to become. To help people see the inner being of a person versus being judged by actions, actions that sometimes were bigger than the people involved, actions that were certainly incomprehensible to a

1

KEENAN HUDSON

kid. The person versus the shadow they cast.

It's no secret that when I was 15, I was involved in a robbery that turned fatal. One of the other guys involved took out a gun and shot the guy we were robbing. It was all over the newspapers and television. He wasn't supposed to use the gun. It certainly wasn't in the plan. But, I was holding the guy we were robbing when my accomplice pulled out a gun and shot the pizza delivery guy in the head, and so I was an accomplice. I am not making excuses. I take full responsibility for my actions, and I apologize to the man who my accomplice killed that night.

The purpose of this book is not to rehash that night, although I will recount what happened. The purpose is to show how it is possible to atone, learn, and rewrite the life I was given, and go on to create a productive life after being part of such a tragedy.

Chapter 1

Growing up

Philadelphia was not the easiest place to grow up.

My mom is Bernetta Hudson, known as Tina, and she is probably the main reason I am not playing the part that was written for me at this point in time. My mom was beloved in the community. She was active in the Incarnation of Our Lord Church in Philadelphia with Sister Pat, a skinny Caucasian lady with grey hair. At Christmas, Sister Pat would send a Santa Claus to our house twice 'cause she liked my mom. My mom was always helping people, helping drug addicts. Giving them food on a plate, which they would bring back the next day. That's how much they respected her.

My father, Kevin Hudson, was a drummer, and he left when I was four. He was consumed by the streets during the crack pandemic and moved to New York where he was incarcerated, and I didn't have much contact with him until I was a teenager. So, it was basically up to my mother to raise me, my brother, and my sister.

KEENAN HUDSON

My older brother's name is Kevin, Jr. My sister's name is Tonette.

I had a big family that was around all the time: two aunts, two uncles. My grandmom had a host of brothers and sisters, and she had five kids so there were a lot of cousins—first, second, and third—and I grew up surrounded by last names like McBride, Allen, and Parker. A lot of my grandmom's siblings—I think there were ten of them—were in Jacksonville, Florida and Sumter, South Carolina. But a lot of them were up here in Philadelphia.

There was a lot of family, but there was no role model for me. My mother's brother, my Uncle Chuckie, was caught up in the streets on drugs. Her other brother, Uncle Eddie, was legit, but he was always working. He was really busy. They never mistreated me, but they weren't role models.

My mom's family was tightknit. The brothers and sisters would take turns watching the kids when one of the adults was at work. One of my favorite cousins was Bianca. She and I were always cool, close to each other. She was the closest to me of all the girl cousins. All my boy cousins looked up to me and loved me despite my growing up as the family black sheep. I always had a lot going on, I was adventurous, playing sports, video games, or cool kid stuff.

I was the black sheep because I was always into something. I had ADHD because I had outrageous problems keeping still, and two of my aunts would beat and punish me more than they beat their own kids. If it was my mom punishing me, I could understand. But it was my Aunt Brenda and my Aunt Bert who were mean to me. My mom knew the way my aunts were to me.

Even though it was a difficult place to grow up, we had plenty of

THE UNSPOKEN TRUTH

fun. I can remember playing Freeze Tag, Catch a Girl, Freak a Girl, Wheelies on Bicycles. We went to the park a lot. In fact, I was never around the house unless my mom made me come in. I played football and basketball for the Olney Eagles. My first basket was a milk crate before my mom was able to get me a real basket and backboard.

We lived in the north part of Philadelphia in the Logan section. It's predominately Afro-American and Puerto Rican now, and there is a lot of poverty which makes it an insecure place as far as crime is concerned. Poverty is always dangerous for the people living in it, not a lot of security.

I can recall the house getting robbed several times when I was a kid. My dad had left, and besides an aunt who sometimes stayed in the back room, mom was alone. It was the crack era and it was easier for crackheads to break into a household without a man. They would take money and jewelry, video games, etc.

My mom bought a row house on 5TH and Rockland Street. She was the first person in her family to own a house. She paid it off, and she worked hard to keep it. She worked as a nurse, she worked at the Acme, she worked as a crossing guard—she used to push my little sister to work in a stroller—and then she worked as a prison guard. Sometimes we had to rely on foodbanks, even after she and my stepfather, Danny Romero, got together. He was Puerto Rican (Boricua) from Rio Piedras and very handy, very creative. He moved in with us with his kids, Jonathan and Dianna. They didn't speak much English at first, but they learned English from us. Because of him I got a host of aunts and uncles who spoke Spanish, which would help me later in jail and then when I got out and worked in a meat packing plant.

KEENAN HUDSON

My mom met my stepfather when she was working as a crossing guard and his family lived across the street from where she worked. She quickly became friends with his sisters, Tia Lucy and Tia Eli. Eli's husband was (RIP) Tio Junior. Lucy's husband was Tio Macho, and Tia Cindy was Macho's and Lucy's daughter-in-law. Tia Cindy's son was my godbrother/cousin, Angel Rivera. He had two sisters, my little cousins Nina and Natasha. They translated for their grandmother because she didn't speak English. A big family, a lot of other kids, too. I can remember the parties that Tia Lucy, Tia Eli, and Tio Jr. (the big dog) would throw almost every day from three in the afternoon till three or four in the morning. A big cookout with music, dancing, and great food. Tia Lucy could cook anything—*arroz con habichuelas, pernil arroz, arroz con gandules, mofongo, pasteles, arroz con dulce.* They used to make rum cakes. My mom would never allow me to eat the rum cakes because of the alcohol in them. We danced to salsa, *bachata*, and *merengue*. This is where my Spanish started picking up. We were learning the different cultures because our families were mingling. We all grew up together.

My mom was always taking care of the kids. We had a houseful of kids, a houseful of boys, so we were always fighting. If my mom didn't have to carry the burden of the whole family, we probably would have gotten a lot further financially, but we were doing better than most.

My brother Kevin and I fought a lot. We couldn't even be in the same room. He was very selfish. My mom said she didn't know where that came from. We had to have two of everything because he wouldn't share—two televisions, two beds, two radios, two remote controls. We couldn't play the same video games. He worked at McDonalds and wouldn't share any of the food he brought home either. He's very

THE UNSPOKEN TRUTH

intelligent and studied a lot and went to one of the top schools in Philadelphia, Central High. When my mother passed, he was getting ready to go to college, Bloomsburg University, which he did at the end of the next semester when he graduated high school. He now works at a big pharmaceutical company.

The street we lived on, Rockland, had a lot of nice people. Miss Nelly, a nurse who was friends with my mother, lived next-door with her husband, Mr. Tony, and kids. The kid I remember the most is Tiny because she was so beautiful. We all liked Tiny. Miss Nelly's house was more stable than ours. Everything seemed to be organized. They would put on events, like an arcade in the basement, lots of family gatherings. They had a basketball court in the backyard. Our house, by comparison, was ghetto—things thrown all over the place, mostly because me and my brother were always fighting and throwing things at each other. We'd throw things out the window trying to hit each other, and a couple of times we hit Miss Nelly's windows instead, but our families stayed friends. Mr. Tony was real handy and he tried to teach me things. They even had a dog that looked like Lassie, a sheep dog that was real friendly,

Mr. Rodney lived across the street with his wife and son. He was cool, old school. He and his wife took a liking to me and not my brother because my brother kept to himself, and I was always out there getting into things. Mr. Rodney was kind of like a cool OG to me, showing me things and taking me places like the barber shop, playing basketball with me.

Miss Rosa lived next door to Mr. Rodney. She was the block captain—whenever there was to be a block cleanup, she would get it organized and get it done. She was like the block grandmother. She lived with her daughter Miss Evelyn and Miss Evelyn's son, Luis, who was my friend. We were friends when I was about nine or ten years old. I stole a couple of things from Luis, like his allowance of $3.56 which was sitting on a table, but once I stole a video game from him. I didn't think he noticed or told anyone and I went home, but later that evening my mom called me downstairs. "Keenan, come down here, please. I want to talk to you." When I came down, Ms. Evelyn was there and my mother was holding one of those weightlifter belts, you know, the ones that are about 10 inches wide. She asks me, "Did you take anything from this house?" When I said that I did, she gave me the worst ass-whipping she ever gave me. She wore my ass out. I never stole anything from Luis again.

Still, my mom tried to look out for me. I was hyperactive, always into something, always creating something. I had a sound studio in my room and a basketball court in the back yard. I was the favorite cousin because I was always doing something. I was always taking small jobs, cutting bushes, moving stuff. When I got a job in a car lot, mom made me be on time, early even. "You be waiting out there before they come in," she would say. She told me I should always be asking what else I could do when I was finished my own work. If I got in trouble at work and she heard about it, she would let them whip my behind if it turned out I was wrong.

The thing is, my mom was friends with everyone in our neighborhood, everyone loved and respected her, and I got a lot of breaks because of her. People were willing to overlook bad behavior on my part because of who my mother was, and she was always moving me to different schools, trying to keep me from getting in trouble in the neighborhood.

I started school in daycare from when I was a baby until I was four

THE UNSPOKEN TRUTH

years old in Ms. Watson's Daycare. After that my mom took me to Incarnation for elementary school. I had kindergarten with Ms. Cline. When I got to first grade, I had my favorite teacher, Ms. Lopez. She was beautiful with long, dark curly hair. I learned more from her than from any other teacher. She was one of my best teachers ever. The other teachers would say, "You have Keenan Hudson next year, Look out!" but Ms. Lopez didn't listen to that. She and my mom were best friends. They loved and cherished each other. She often spoke highly of me and my brother and still loves us to this day.

But my incredible energy also meant that I was always annoying people in authority. My mom knew and she tried to talk to me. She would never put me down, she would be understanding of my uncontrollable energy. It seemed I was powerless to stop. I had issues in school, always an outcast. She took me to doctors, and they diagnosed me as having ADHD. They gave me Ritalin just to keep me quiet. I hated Ritalin. It messes with your hormones and your appetite. It kept me real slouchy all day. Half the time I tried to spit it out if I thought I wouldn't get caught. Of course, now, in 2022, they have had years to study the effects of this drug on kids[1] and a lot of the long-term effects are not good, but then they were giving it out like candy to control kids, mostly boys, who were overactive.

When I look back on it now, if my mind had been occupied with something that interested and challenged me—I was a smart kid and easily bored—my mom said I rode a bike at four without training wheels, just like Jay-Z—I probably would have sat still to learn, but there was no

---

[1] https://www.cchrflorida.org/children-on-ritalin-long-term-effects/

KEENAN HUDSON

one around who could cope with me, much less figure out what I needed to thrive.[2] That's a luxury only the kids of rich parents have.

Between my mom's house and my grandma's neighborhood I had a lot of so-called friends. Between the ages of 7 and 10, I was out on the streets a lot. I was getting in trouble, getting in fights on the way to school, and my mom said she didn't want to waste money sending me to Catholic school. But she didn't want to send me to a neighborhood school where I would get into trouble, so she finally sent me to Hope Christian Academy. That was my first experience with morning and noon day service. They played music like a church service but at school. I wound up getting into trouble there, so I was only there for a year before I was kicked out for fighting. I was in fifth grade by this time.

Because my mom didn't want me to go to school in the neighborhood, she used my Aunt Bert's address on Allengrove Street in northeast Philly to get me into Creighton Elementary School. It was a public school, and there I got a TSS worker—a wraparound—which kind of kept me in check, but I still got in fights anyway.

I stayed in Creighton Elementary School till 7th grade, and when it was time to go to 8th grade, I went to Thurgood Marshall Middle School. I was like an outcast there. I was quiet, and when they saw you were quiet they would pick on you and try to get their friends to pick on you. I had fun for a while. I was messing around with girls. I had my first girlfriend, Shaheita. Our grandparents lived on the same block. I was into the music. I was burning CDs on my computer. I was into fashion, wearing Gebo

---

[2] I write about this in another book, *The Incarceration of the Juvenile Mind.* Check out my website for release date and how to order.

THE UNSPOKEN TRUTH

jeans. I still got into a lot of fights, though, my mom got called to pick me up lots of times. I graduated, but only because they were pushing me through.

When it came time to pick a high school to go to, the only schools that accepted me were all neighborhood schools: Olney High School, Fels High School, and Martin Luther King High School. My mom knew I would get in trouble in all of those schools and didn't know what to do until one day she ran into my cousin, Wayne "Wiz" Allen (football legend, Philadelphia Aztecs). He was 33 years old at the time. He said, "Let me make a couple of calls." I was a big guy and he thought I could play football in a school in a better neighborhood. He contacted the head football coach, Ron Cohen, of George Washington High School in northeast Philly. So, my mom, me, Ron Cohen, and the principal of George Washington High School, Alan Liebowitz, had a meeting. They pulled some strings and allowed me to attend George Washington High School as a football player. They were very welcoming, saying, "We definitely hope the best for you."

I couldn't play football that year because tryouts had passed. I was still getting into fights, but I only had two fights in the high school. I was getting into fights in the neighborhood.

It was right around this time that my mom was getting sick. I wasn't sure what was going on with her because no one would tell me anything. First of all, I was only 13 years old when she got sick. She was in the hospital and when I went to see her, I kept saying, "when you get out," and "when you get better and come home." But nobody told me that she wasn't getting better and she wasn't coming home except to die, She was diagnosed with cancer.

KEENAN HUDSON

It was right before Christmas. I told her I wanted a motorbike for when I graduated to high school. My aunt Brenda laughed at me, but nobody told me why it was ridiculous. They covered it up for a long time, saying she was sick but was going to get better. Really, no one talked about it.

My mom had been in the hospital, but she came back home, and I thought she was getting better. I didn't know and no one told me that she came home because there was nothing else they could do for her in the hospital.

> My mom passed at age 41 on the 28th of December, 2002.

THE UNSPOKEN TRUTH

Dear Mom

I'm thankful that you have been there for me,
I've always loved your smile that I could see for miles and miles,
I know that you are in heaven and I will be there one day,
I know that you are with me even though you are away,
I know that you are with me every single day,
I have family and others, but there is nothing like having a mother.
Love You,
Your son, Keenan

Best Friends For Life
Mom, I will always remember you. I love you and I know you love me
too, you're more than a mother to me. You were my best friend.
I know you had to go when God called because you're a wonderful,
kind and loving person.
Love You Always,
Your "Netty Bett" (Tonette)

Mother,
Here she stands, my mother for seventeen years. As I look at her, I
sense that someone has wound that clock. Years has become
increments. History has a beginning and an end. Then Mother's arms
wrap me in warmth, and I am home. A seventeen old child reassured
by his mother's touch. There is no time in touch I will miss you Mom.
Love,
Your son, Kevin

Aunt Tee-Tee
I had fun with you aunt Tee-Tee and I know God had to take you
home. I will always remember and love you. I will not forget how you
cheered me up when I was sad.
Love,
Your "Love Bug"
Janae'

My Aunt Tee Tee
Remember our sleep over, just you and me. Tonetta and Lil Mama.
Remember the laughter we all shared. I will always remember that
smile. I know you are in heaven and smiling down.

Love,
Boo-Boo

Chapter 2

Alone in The House After My Mother Passed

My whole world changed when my mom passed.

In some ways, death isn't real to kids. It's hard to imagine that someone who was just there talking to you isn't there anymore. When she passed, my Aunt Brenda was named the legal guardian of me and my brother and she was supposed to take care of the house until we were old enough to take it over. She moved in with her partner and her kids and grandkids. He was okay, but I didn't really pay him no mind.

After my Aunt Brenda moved in, my stepfather moved out. Kevin was getting ready to go to Bloomsburg University. Jonathan had already moved out and was living with his girlfriend, now wife, Angie. Dianna went back to Puerto Rico. Aaron, my foster brother, was already living in another foster home. My aunt Bert took custody of Tonette.

My aunt's kids were always going through my stuff, so I put a padlock on my door which caused a lot of drama. We weren't supposed to have secrets, but I was becoming a teenager and I needed my privacy.

I was increasingly isolated and, really, I was the only one of my family left in what was supposed to be my house.

I started working on music, forming a little rap group with my

THE UNSPOKEN TRUTH

friends. I remember what my grandmom used to say, though: "Kennan, you don't have friends. Those boys aren't your friends." So, I was kind of alone.

My father had just started cleaning up and had moved to New York. My aunt didn't like me hanging around in my locked room with my friends, so she was only too happy to put me on the bus to New York to be with my dad. I had never spent much time with my father. I knew he was a drummer, that was it, but from what I knew of him, he'd changed. He started going to church, and he ended up being a building superintendent. NY was great, but he was boring. I tried to go out, but he wouldn't let me, so that experiment didn't last long.

I remember when I came back, my uncle was mad that I came back. "The King is home," he would say sarcastically. "The King, The King, The King!" Things were always cooking when I was home, and kids were always around. The kids loved me, so yeah, I was the King.

During this time, my aunt was sending me to school, and they couldn't afford to spend much on me. They sent me to school in British Nikes and Converses, off brands that weren't the fad at the time, because I didn't have money to afford the good stuff like everyone else. I couldn't go on school trips. Everyone made fun of me, because they had stuff, and I didn't. I felt really empty-handed and lonely.

Some of the people I was hanging with, like James my best friend, introduced me to smoking weed. In the morning, we'd meet up at the bus station where we'd buy a five dollar bag. Pretty soon, it went from me having a couple of puffs to me buying my own bag. Eventually I was buying ounces for 80 dollars. Needless to say, my grades starting slipping to Ds and Fs.

15

KEENAN HUDSON

I didn't smoke all the weed. I sold some of it and doubled my money. I used to go to this store, Sunshine Blues, and buy new sneakers and new jeans, not just buy, we used to steal stuff, put stuff in our book bags. That's where my entrepreneurship started. White and black t-shirts were very popular back then, different sizes, 4x mostly, people liked big t-shirts, 5x, 6x. I used to go to a wholesale store with a duffle bag. The guy who owned it had a box of defective t-shirts he sold for 50 cents. They weren't defective enough to be noticeable, but he couldn't sell them for full price. I bought those t-shirts—black and white t-shirts on the street were going to 5 dollars, free sizes, past your knees, for 6 dollars.

Besides the t-shirts, I would buy firecrackers for a dollar at the Dollar Store. I sold them for twice the amount. They had these little weird sex key chains. I would buy two for 1 dollar and sell them for 2. I got a big Worge fur jacket. One thing about me, I didn't care about the name brand. People thought I spent a lot of money on my clothes and things, but I didn't.

I had a big knot of money, mostly ones. Perception. Illusion. Same as on Facebook and Instagram. Perception. Illusion. You keep the fives on the outside of the knot and the ones inside.

I tried out and made the George Washington football team the next year, in 2003. I played a couple of games, tackle and nose guard. I remember training very hard with a team captain named Jason Patton who was a senior and a monster on the football field. He would always push us to the limit, and some of us used to hide in the bathroom until the hard drills were over. After practice, a group of us would get on the 58 Septa bus and act the fool, cracking jokes on people on the bus and each other. We were some troublesome kids.

THE UNSPOKEN TRUTH

Often I found myself getting sent to detention for acting up in class, and I had to face the strict but loving deans of the school, Miss Hughes, Miss Sudler, and Miss Wright. "You're here again! How many times do we have to tell you, you gotta behave." The best algebra teacher, Mr. Lopez, would correct me at times. I kept acting up, but I never disrespected him. George Washington was a positive experience for me. These were good people who wished me well.

I wound up with a group of teammates on a Septa bus that got into an accident, and we couldn't play anymore because we put in a lawsuit against Septa. I recall taking the R train to Frankford, which was the hub for a lot of schools. I was still going to games, supporting the team, but my friends and I were like a flash mob, running into stores, stealing things. I wound up dropping out and going to night school. It was the same school, but I went from three in the afternoon till six. It wasn't a big time difference, and eventually I transferred back to regular school. It felt like everything was happening all at once.

My aunt would try to send me to a group home because she couldn't control me. My aunt would say, "I'm not feeding you," but of course she had to.

When my mom passed away, she had life insurance. When I was young, I would hear things, even if I didn't always know what they meant. I knew she had $100,000 in life insurance, and I remember seeing an itinerary of where the money should go. But my aunt kept it all, and she was blowing the money. She wasn't paying the taxes on the house. I was already incarcerated by the time my brother came home from spring break and found an eviction notice on the front door. She had lost the house after just two years. He had to go to my grandmother's house and sleep on the floor. He said, "Once I finish college, I'm not coming back." I can't blame him. Me and my brother talk now and then. He has a good job with a big pharmaceutical company and a big house. We could be closer, but our lives took such different paths and for so long, we have a long way to get back together. The only other person in our family he talks to is Uncle Eddie, my mother's brother.

I would do anything to get money. I used to shovel snow. My grandma would tell me if her friends needed weeds wacked or bushes cut. Anything I could do for money. My grandma would give me five dollars to keep quiet all day. I would always get my grandma to save the money for me. She would save their money for other people, too, which I didn't know at the time. One time, this guy, AB, came and gave my grandma some money. She went to the china cabinet and put it in there. Sometimes my aunts would take my money, and they would get mad when I wanted it back.

I'd been hanging around my grandma's house a lot more. I met some guys, four guys my homie Brian introduced me to. We clicked right away. Chillin'. Hanging out. Playing basketball. And doing stupid stuff as usual. My homie got into trouble in another neighborhood and went to placement. Placement is like a group home for boys for reconditioning— you do something crazy, and you go to juvenile court, then you get sent away.

I was already in high school. I was always plotting something, mostly how to make money. I always had money, and I was never hungry 'cause my grandma cooked every night, but I was hanging with these kids. As I explain in my book, *The Incarceration of the Juvenile Mind*, peer pressure plays a big part in a teenage boy's life. I was no exception. When

THE UNSPOKEN TRUTH

someone in the group suggests something, even if you know it's wrong or even if you'd just rather not, you don't want them to think you're scared and you have to prove yourself, so you go along.

So, when Martique, we called him Marty, said we should order from a pizza parlor, then rob the delivery guy and steal his car, we all said, "Let's plan this thing out." The whole motive was to get the money and the car. That was the plan.

For me, it was falling to the temptation of peer pressure. Because I didn't need the money, and no matter how the newspapers and the television stations dramatized it later, I wasn't hungry.

Photo Album of My Family

Group photo of the McBride family in the 1980s, Left to right: Aunt Brenda, Mom, Uncle Eddie, Uncle Chuckie, Mom-Mom, Pop-Pop, Aunt Bert.

My father, Kevin Hudson, his sister, my aunt Valerie, and Uncle Ronald, visiting me in prison.

My mother, Bernetta "Tina" Hudson.

Left, my younger sister Tonette. Below left, me and my older brother, Kevin, Jr.

Below right, me on the Olney Eagles team.

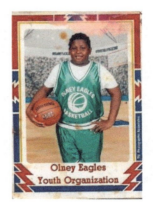

My Stepfamily

My stepfather, Danny Romero

Tia Eli, Danny's sister

Tia Lucy and her grandchildren

Abuela Maria

My mom, seated in background, Tio Macho, Lucy's husband, my step-brother Jonathan, and my cousin-godbrother baby Angel Rivera who was brutally murdered in 2021.

Tio Jr., Eli's husband, who died. He was a good man and a big influence on me.

Chapter 3

How It Went Down

This is how it went down.

There were five of us—Marty, Justin, Van, Stephan, and me. I had a friend who lived in a house down the hill from where we were gonna rob the pizza delivery guy. It was kind of out of the way, lots of trees. We gave the pizza place a phone number of Marty's relatives in Port Richmond, another part of Philadelphia. Marty told them if someone from the pizza store called, tell them they ordered it and go ahead and deliver it. We thought that way, they couldn't trace the call to one of us.

So, Marty was behind the bushes, Justin was across the street at the bus stop, Steph was on the steps, and Van was on his bike by a tree. I was standing right in front of the house where the guy was going stop.

The delivery guy got out of his car. When he went towards the steps, I came up behind him and bear hugged him. The car engine was running. Steph was supposed to get in the car and take off, but he got scared and ran away. But when I got the delivery guy in a bear hug, Marty pulled a gun out and held it to the guy's head. I was holding the guy with one arm and going through his pockets with the other. He didn't have much money on him, only change, a bunch of quarters, nickels, dimes, and pennies The guy didn't resist at all, he didn't say anything, he was

THE UNSPOKEN TRUTH

shaking. He surrendered everything. Take it all, he said.

Marty was wound up, holding the gun at him and yelling. Then suddenly, for no reason at all, Marty shot the guy in the head.

Steph, Justin, Marty, and me all ran to Justin's house up the hill. Van was who was the lookout jumped on his bicycle and took off.

When we got to Justin's house, even though the guy was laying in the street back there, Steph said, "Let's get the food and eat."

I can honestly say I didn't even know what was happening. Here, Marty just shot a man in the head, and Steph wants to eat? It was crazy!

I said, "Here, take all this money, I want none of this stuff, I'm out of here."

I heard sirens, and I ran to my grandma's house. I had to zigzag to get to her house. She lived exactly one block from where the shooting happened. I was in shock. I turned on the TV and checked the news. It was already on all the Philly news channels: "Delivery man shot! The murderer is still on the loose."

I couldn't sleep all night. The next morning I went to school. Of course, everything was all over the news, but no one was talking about me, so I thought I was okay.

The police were just starting their investigation. I didn't find out the particulars until later when I saw the discovery package that included everything from statements to biopsy to lab reports.

They began by tracing all the phone calls. They were able to trace the *67 calls that we thought were blocked. They traced the number to Marty's relatives in Port Richmond. The police raided their house, kicked the door in. They said they didn't know anything more than what Martique told them. It was through them that they located Marty.

KEENAN HUDSON

What happened took place on March 28th. Martique was captured on April 1.

By this time I went back to my home in Logan. My cousin told me there was a rumor going around high school that Marty and Biggs—Biggs was my nickname—were the ones who killed the guy. I kept on acting like I didn't know what was going on. Like I didn't know anything about it.

After about a week and a half later, Marty's relatives went to see my grandma. Our families grew up together. They knocked on her door and they said "We have to talk about something."

My grandma says, "What's going on?"

They said, "Listen. The pizza man who got killed the other night, Marty is telling the cops that your grandson pulled the trigger. Biggs did it. Martique is in custody. He's saying Biggs did it."

My grandma tells my Uncle Eddie who is my legal guardian and who was always lecturing me about staying out late, coming in the house late. He comes to my house. Already three weeks have gone by so I thought it was over. There were kids in my room. My Uncle Eddie tells them to leave and says to me, "Keenan, I got something to ask you. Were you involved in the killing of that pizza man? The boys who were involved are telling the cops, you're the one who did it." But I played it off, like I didn't know anything.

Grandma who would come to my house every morning told my aunt there was a police car parked at the corner of her house.

I had no contact with any of the others (to be continued in Who Ratted on Who). By now, it's around April 10, and a full-blown investigation is going on. When they started saying it was me who was involved, I knew they were telling the cops everything, including that it

THE UNSPOKEN TRUTH

was me who pulled the trigger, despite me denying everything, because the cops knew way too much. The only way they could know everything is if the other guys were talking.

My Uncle Eddie said, "We got to find Keenan a lawyer."

Chapter 4

My Lawyer

At this time, my aunt Brenda and my Uncle Eddie still had some of my mom's insurance money, so they were able to hire a lawyer for me, Burton A. Rose, in downtown Philadelphia on Spring Garden St.

A meeting was scheduled to meet him. Literally, my whole family—uncles, aunts, great aunts, about 25 people came to the lawyer's office to support me. They had to take us to a big conference room with a double table to fit all of us. And this is just my family: grandma's sisters, blood relatives, my dad's sister. They didn't know me as a street person, and I think they found it hard to believe this was happening to me.

The lawyer sized us up and took me from the room. "I need to talk to Keenan alone," he said.

My uncle pulled me aside before I left the room. "If he thinks you're lying, Keenan, he won't represent you."

I was already going over alibis in my head.

Mr. Rose pulled me in a room with him and his secretary, Claire. "Listen, Keenan," he said. "We got details of things that went down." He had a good ear to the legal street, if you know what I mean. "For us to represent you well, I need the truth."

Naturally, I gave him an alibi. "I was in my grandma's house. I heard a shot," I said.

He knew I was lying. He said, "Keenan, I don't feel that you're being

THE UNSPOKEN TRUTH

totally honest with me. I'm trying to help you. These guys aren't your friends."

Right then, I knew they knew everything. I told Mr. Rose, "I played a part, but I didn't shoot the guy in the head. I just held him and took change from his pocket." I gave Mr. Rose the whole story clean.

Mr. Rose said, "Okay. I'm going to process this and figure out the best thing to do."

A few days later he came up with a decision. We have to go down to the roundhouse where they keep homicide suspects. They processed me, took my picture, name, and description to see if my identity matched what the other guys were saying, to make sure it was not mistaken identity.

A week later, the other guys were shown my picture and they said, "Hey, that's Biggs." Mr. Rose told me, "Listen, they identified you. You can do one of two things. You can stay on the street till they come get you or you can turn yourself in."

My family gave me the option. It's up to you, whatever you want to do. I had one week to decide.

I was trying to decide what to do and I was watching prison movie— Comcast, digital cable. What should I do? I wasn't talking to anybody. I watched *Holes*, a movie about juveniles locked up in a desert detention camp. I came to the conclusion that if I ran, eventually they're going to catch me, eventually I'm going to be locked up, so I decided to turn myself in. I believed it was the right thing to do. Someone had been murdered, and it overshadowed my heart with regret and remorse.

The first article *The Metropolitan* wrote about me: Police arrested a suspect in the pizza delivery man murder. That was the very first article.

31

KEENAN HUDSON

They said I was arrested in my home. That's when I realized that they could say anything they wanted to, even if it was a lie.

Chapter 5

My Arrest

The crime took place March 28th. I was arrested April 26th. I was 15 years old.

There were 20 people supporting me when I turned myself in at the Roundhouse, at 8th and Race St. I gave my family hugs, said goodbye, then I went in with my lawyer. They charge people with homicides on the third floor which they call the Homicide Unit. The first doors I walked through led me to a desk with a chair which had a handcuff on it. I had a little Bible with me that my grandma told me, take it with you.

I was reading the Bible when the investigator came into the room and asked me, "What happened." Mr. Rose had left.

I said, "I can't talk without my attorney here."

The investigator said, "No problem. It looks like you're going to jail for the rest of your life." He was trying to intimidate me, but I was too strong minded to respond so he left the interrogation room.

Later that night I had an arraignment hearing by a judge.

I was initially charged with first degree murder, criminal conspiracy, concealed firearms, robbery, carrying firearms without a license, and possession of an instrument of crime. They stack the charges. Murder

KEENAN HUDSON

carries life sentence/death penalty. The charges that were stacked could run consecutively (which is called running wild) or concurrently. You get a certain sentence for each charge. Consecutively means once you complete one sentence you start the next sentence, meaning I'd be looking at life in prison. Concurrently means all sentences running at the same time, so I would only have to serve the longest sentence.

When you're charged with murder, you're held with zero bond, no bail even as a juvenile. During the court procedures, you're in the CJC, Criminal Justice Center. They run evaluations of all kinds – psychological, physical, getting your whole history.

I was in the Roundhouse for 24 hours. Then I was sent to the House of Corrections located on State Road.

In the county jail, they tell you to strip naked and put all your clothes in a box. You were only allowed to have your t-shirt, boxers, and socks. Then they do a strip search, which is you turn your palms up, lift your feet, bend over and spread your cheeks, squat and cough, lift your balls. Then they throw you in the shower with antibiotic soap to get rid of scabies if you have them or any other contagious bacterial germs.

When you come out of the shower, they put you in an orange jump suit. They have two uniforms—The Blues, sky blue shirt, navy blue pants, which means you were part of the population and Orange, representing that you were in the hole or quarantine. I was given orange because all intakes are on 7 days quarantine. I was in the juvenile block which housed guys who were 12-17 years old.

I was in quarantine for the 7 days. We had gate-like cells, so you could always see into other cells or throw something in. Someone threw a piece of paper into my cell one day shortly after I was there. "Hey, big

34

THE UNSPOKEN TRUTH

guy, check this out." It was a balled-up newspaper. I wasn't insulted being called big guy, because at 15 I was already 6 feet tall and weighed 300 pounds. My cellmate picked up the paper. It was a newspaper article about me. The press put a spin on it, they said I did it because I was hungry, I wanted some food. That's just not how it happened, but I didn't react so anyone could see. Whenever someone says something that's meant to insult you, that's when the fights start.

I was supposed to be alone, but I was in with three other guys. That's considered cruel and unusual punishment (violation of the 8th Amendment), by the way. If they found you had some kind of medical problem after you had a medical exam, you were in there longer.

Teen guilty of murder in slaying of pizza deliveryman

By THERESA CONROY
conroyt@phillynews.com

Wearing a white dress shirt and black trousers sinking way below his hips, the hulking criminal — not yet old enough to drive a car — ambled into Common Pleas Court yesterday and admitted his part in the brutal robbery and murder of a pizza deliveryman this spring.

Keenan Hudson, 15, pleaded guilty to third-degree murder and conspiracy to rob Abraham Cisse on March 28.

Under his plea agreement, the Philadelphia district attorney's office will recommend Hudson be sentenced to 12½ to 25 years in prison. Hudson has agreed to testify against co-defendant Martique Daughtry, 16.

The only thing the 6-foot-5-inch defendant added to yesterday's brief proceeding — aside from the obvious sadness felt by his relatives in court — was a denial to witness statements pointing him as the mastermind behind the bogus pizza order that lured Cisse to his death.

"Martique planned everything out, and he was going to tell peo-ple where to go and what to do, and I was in on it," Hudson told Judge Benjamin Lerner.

Cisse, a West African immi-grant, was shot in the head dur-ing the West Oak Lane robbery. He died the next day.

Daughtry, who confessed to shooting Cisse, was held for trial in May on murder and robbery charges.

Another teen allegedly involved in the plot, Justin Frazier, 17, has been granted immunity to testify against Daughtry.

Hudson, called "Bigs" due to his huge build, wanted some food and money, so the teens got the phone number for Papa's Perfect Pizza, in Cedarbrook, from a pa-per menu, Frazier said during Daughtry's May preliminary hearing. The kids placed an order for two pizzas, two cheesesteaks and 30 wings, according to the earlier testimony.

When Cisse arrived with the food, the teens robbed him of a small amount of cash — about enough to buy a pack of ciga-rettes — and shot him with a .380-caliber semiautomatic pis-tol, police said.

"It was stupid," prosecutor Car-men Lineberger said of the crime.

The immaturity of the defen-dants was never more evident than in the aftermath of the shoot-ing, Lineberger said. After the kill-ing, Frazier said, the teens took the sandwiches and pizza back home but only nibbled on it be-cause the food "wasn't good so ev-erybody threw it away."

A trial date for Daughtry has not been set. ★

35

KEENAN HUDSON

Commonwealth of Pennsylvania

County of Philadelphia

DC #04-14-0~~28728~~
M04-081

Warrant # 282534

AFFIDAVIT
OF
Probable Cause for Arrest Warrant

Affiant: Det.John CAHILL, Badge #919, of Homicide Division, being duly sworn according to law, deposes and says:

1. That after investigation I have probable cause to believe that a warrant of arrest should issue for:

NAME Keenan Demetrius HUDSON 15 yrs, RACE B, SEX MALE,

DOB 01-16-89, PPN_____, OTHER_____

ADDRESS 520 W. Rockland St.,Phila.,PA

charging (crimes): MURDER 2502, Robbery 3701, VUFA 6106, VUFA 6108, PIC 907, Consp 903

2. That the facts tending to establish the grounds for the issuance of the warrant of arrest and the probable cause for my belief are as follows:

On **Sunday 3-28-04** at approx.904pm 14th Dist.Police responded to a radio call "Reports of Gunshots, person shot, **7407 Andrews Ave**". Upon police arrival they found the victim, identified as **Abraham CISSE 26/b/m**, lying on the steps outside 7407 Andrews Ave with a gunshot wound to his head. The victim was transported by Medic 33 to AEMC where he was admitted in critical condition. On Monday, 3-29-04 at 11:45am the victim was pronounced by Dr. Williams.

On 3-30-04, Dr.McDONALD, Assistant Medical Examiner of the Philadelphia Medical Examiners office, supervised an autopsy on the remains of Abraham CISSE and reported that the cause of death was a gunshot wound to the head and then manner of death to be Homicide.

_____ 9 15 Homicide
SIGNATURE OF AFFIANT   BADGE #   DISTRICT/UNIT

Sworn to (or affirmed) and subscribed before me this 26th
day of ____ April ____ 8 2004

_____   (SEAL)
SIGNATURE OF ISSUING AUTHORITY

75-372 (Rev. 1/92)

THE UNSPOKEN TRUTH

CONTINUATION OF AFFIDAVIT OF PROBABLE CAUSE FOR ARREST WARRANT, PAGE #2
DC # <// 04- 14 · 2372)

M#04-081

WAN # 282534

On 3-31-04, Kareem DAUGHTRY 17/b/m, was interviewed by your affiant and he stated in summary that he is the brother to Martique DAUGHTRY and that at approx 7pm on Sunday 3-28-04 he was inside his residence at 1967 74th Ave when he observed his brother MARTY talking with another b/m known to him as "BIGGS" and they were talking about ordering food. He further stated and that on Monday 3-29-04 he spoke with Marty and Marty told him that he and BIGGS robbed and shoot a pizza delivery man on 3-28-04 at 7407 Andrews Ave.

On 4-1-04, Martique DAUGHTRY aka Marty 16/b/m, was arrested and charged with murder and related offenses and he gave a statement after warnings during which he stated that he conspired with "Biggs" to rob the pizza man on 3-28-04 at 7407 Andrews Ave and during the robbery Marty did shot and kill the compl.

On 4-20-04 Robert WHITE 15/b/m, was interviewed by your affiant and he stated in summary that on 3-28-04 he was present at 1967 74th Ave when Martique DAUGHTRY and BIGGS planned the robbery of the pizza man and he further stated that at about 9pm that date he was at 74th and Andrews Ave when he heard a gunshot and then observed both Biggs and Martique Daughtry running away from 7407 Andrews Ave where the compl was murdered. On 4-20-04 White was shown a photo array by Det Lynch #796 which he viewed and positively identified photo #7 as the person he knows as Biggs and this being the same person he observed plan the robbery and the same person he observed fleeing the scene after the shooting.

On 4-21-04, Justin FRAZIER 16/b/m, was interviewed by your affiant and he stated in summary that on 3-28-04 he was present at 1967 74th Ave when Martique DAUGHTRY and BIGGS planned the robbery of the pizza man and he further stated that at about 9pm that date he was at 74th and Andrews Ave when he observed the pizza man arrive outside 7407 Andrews Ave and Biggs grabbed the compl in a bear hug and Marty shot the compl. On 4-21-04 Frazier was shown a photo array by Det Mellon #9029 which he viewed and positively identified photo #7 as the person he knows as Biggs and this being the same person he observed plan the robbery and the same person he observed holding the compl while Martique shot the compl at 7407 Andrews Ave.

Photo #7 is assigned to the subject **Keenan HUDSON** 15/b/m dob:1-16-89 res.520 W. Rockland St.

As a result of the above information which your affiant believes to be true and correct I respectfully request that an arrest warrant be issued for the above subject charging him with the listed offenses.

SIGNATURE OF AFFIANT   BADGE # 9 1 5   Homicide

Sworn to (or affirmed) and subscribed before me this:

day of _____ April 19 8 2xx   DISTRICT UNIT 26

SIGNATURE OF ISSUING AUTHORITY   (SEAL)

75-573 (Rev. 1/83)

When I got off quarantine they moved me to the last cell in the block, next to the hole, with the people I was in quarantine with. Now I was in population. They issued me county blues. If you didn't have shoes, they gave you state skippies, a low cost shoe that you can walk in, but you can't run in them.

KEENAN HUDSON

It was my roughest stop because there was a lot of crap in the air. Hearsay about the crime. Marty was there before me, and he was telling everyone I did it.

At this point, I still didn't know the totality of what was happening to my case. I hadn't yet seen the statements from everyone else involved in the case. During this time, people were coming up to the gate saying, "Hey, what's going? We want to know?" People are curious and envious. Marty was in the general population, too. He'd been talking a lot of shit about the crime, saying I did it, but to my face he denied it. I wanted to beat the crap out of him, but Mr. Rose told me, "Keep your nose clean when you're in there because you don't want to have a dirty jacket." Marty tried to bribe me with commissary cakes and stuff to make me think he was on my side.

I had a May court date scheduled for my preliminary hearing. On the advice of my lawyer I appeared in court and waived it.

I started going to school. I wanted to get my diploma. When we went to school the individuals in the hole came out to shower. The guards left the gates unlocked, and when we got back, we saw that someone had raided our cell. They stole stuff out of our cell. The word was that it was someone named New York. Marty put the word out. They were going to tune him up. That's what happened the very next night, when I was at Bible study. They locked down the jail after they beat up New York. That was Marty's way of saying he was right with me. I tried to ignore the gossip and the rumors by keeping busy, but it was hard.

There was lots of noise. There were 40 cellblocks, 3 to 4 juvies in each one. And juvies like to make noise. Always taunting. Always trying to pick fights.

THE UNSPOKEN TRUTH

Early in the juvenile block, I got into fights. The fights were always about the rumors. People talking shit about me. I got in a lot of fights after my mom had passed. I started learning lessons, you can't get drawn into peer pressure. Of course, I learned that too late. I learned early, though, not to disrespect anyone. When I was first in CJC (Criminal Justice Center) I was separated with other juveniles away from the adults. We could see each other through the cell bars, and we could see the adults who were right across from us. Some of them were already upstate, which means they were already convicted of crimes and were just here awaiting a court date. Knowing that, you would think we would try to ignore the adults who had nothing to lose if they hurt us, but as I said, we were kids.

There was a big guy across from me, and I was making ape motions and noises, taunting him. The big guy went crazy, shaking the bars, screaming at me, but I thought I was safe, because I was behind bars. Later, when they called me for court, the guard took me over to this guy's cell and made like he was going to open the door and push me in. I had never been so scared in my life. The guard didn't push me in, though. He was just trying to teach me a lesson. "Some of these guys are in for three life sentences," he told me. "They're never going home. They have nothing to lose if they beat the shit out of you or even kill you."

That was a big lesson for me. Don't cross that line. Approach everyone with respect. Don't be afraid to humble yourself. I always had it in my mind, I would be free one day. I always thought I would go home.

I was always out of my cell, only in it during count down. I was the block representative, I was the top dog, you got paid to be the block representative. If the guys in the block had a problem with the food or

KEENAN HUDSON

treatment, I was the one who represented them. I ran the block laundry room, I washed the clothes. I was going to school to get my diploma. The school was really bad, though, they would pass people just to say they passed, no one could read or write. I made some money writing letters for guys and tutoring them, writing out their commissary slips. Finally, we heard a rumor that we were going to get a new principal who was going to turn things around—Mr. Hilderbrand Pelzer III.

Mr. Pelzer told us he was going to get laptops for the school. I said no you aren't, but he did. His main objective was to transform school systems for incarcerated juveniles. He's the reason I wrote my first book, *Broken Promises.*

Us juveniles had access to the computers, we used to draw guns and show them shooting people. He told me to go to the hard drive and get rid of that stuff because I was very good with computers, What really stuck out for me one day was when the school board was coming to the prison. He had created a student Second Chance Room where, if one of us got kicked out of class, we could still go there to do our work. So when he found out the school board was coming, he told me, "I want you present in the room. I'm going to appoint you to show them what happens here." It's always stuck with me that he picked me to lead. He told us, no matter where we were now, we could still do things with our lives. That stuck with me, too.

School and work were the good parts. The bad part was that I almost lost my life. Once I was trying to break two friends up, saying "chill, chill" and someone pulled a knife on me. Play fights in the cell sometimes turned serious. In one fight I was in a headlock, I fell and smacked face down on the floor. They thought I was dead.

THE UNSPOKEN TRUTH

And the bullshit about the murder didn't stop. The case was unveiling in the courts. Me and Marty got into it because he hadn't stopped telling people I killed the guy. We had to be in the hole until they figured out what to do with us, two separate blocks. I wound up getting in fights because people were disrespecting me. I got jumped a couple of times. People calling me a rat, me trying to defend my name. Marty and I could see each other through the cell bars. They finally created a court order to permanently separate us. Mostly though, it wasn't a physical challenge. It was a mental challenge.

My lawyer, Mr. Rose, said that with the evidence they had and all the witness statements they knew who the two main accomplices were, his point being that everyone has made statements against me. However, the police knew Marty was the shooter and you were the one who bear hugged the victim. Knowing that Marty, his brother, his cousin, and other witnesses, had made statements against me, my lawyer said there was no way out of this for me. Therefore, a plea deal was being offered to me, Murder in the 3rd Degree –12 ½ -25 years—on the condition that if it came down to Marty going to trial, I would have to testify against him.

See Appendix, page 90, for key statements (who ratted on who) in full that led to Probable Cause affidavit for Keenan Hudson's arrest.

Chapter 6

Who Ratted on Who

With all the gossip and bullshit about the crime that was swirling around the jail, especially after my guilty plea, I never got a chance to tell the real story of who ratted on who. Because I followed a policy of keeping my mouth shut and keeping to myself, it was easy for others to make themselves look good by lying about me. I want to explain what was happening in the investigation before the cops and DA even got to me.

When you're a kid, you're constantly given information on how to fit in. Some of the stuff is material: you have to wear a certain type of clothing, listen to certain artists. Some of it is behavioral: you have to act for the good of the group, the integrity of the group. No one outside the group should know what goes on inside the group. The worst thing you could do is snitch: rat out someone in the group. Ratting out a homie is a no-no because by choosing your own safety over a homie's you're destroying the group.

This is what people call the street code. It's part of urban culture. Never tell under any circumstance. Even if you are being falsely accused, you never tell on your friends. If your next-door neighbor commits a crime, when the cops question him, and he accuses you, Yo! you still

KEENAN HUDSON

don't talk. Everybody counts on you not to talk. You're not saying anything 'cause you're a so-called gangsta. That's the street code. But as I found out, I was operating on one system of values and the others involved in the crime were operating on another. My so-called friends who I trusted were pointing the finger and telling on me. This is the reason why I accepted the plea deal.

The crime happened on March 28th, and as you can see by the timeline of events, I held out talking until it became obvious that everyone involved was singing and most of it was bullshit to save their skin and hang me because I wasn't defending myself.

My lawyer got ahold of the case, and he was talking to the detectives. He showed me their statements, all typed up and signed. All documented. And at first, they were all trying to say it was me.

This is the statements timelines that led up to my guilty plea. The first person they questioned was Shaheed Haith on March 29th. Shaheed was a childhood friend of mine. He called the cops to tell them he saw a man on the ground bleeding from his head. But he said he didn't know anything else about it.

On the same day, the cops were talking to Martique's family in Port Richmond, because they'd traced the *69 call that we thought was blocked. The cops raided them, but they told the cops they didn't know anything except that Martique told them to tell the pizza place that they ordered the food in case they called to confirm.

From there, the cops got to Martique's brother, Kareem. On March 29th and on March 31st, he made two statement based on everything he remembered that night.

The police talked to Martique on April 1, the day after they talked

THE UNSPOKEN TRUTH

to his brother. This is what opened the whole case up. They questioned Marty, can he read and write? Yeah. Before he went there, he was already talking to his family about what happened. He said he shot the pizza man. Before that, he was telling everyone I did it. He told everyone in the high school that Biggs did it. Martique said he took the gun from Kareem and was with Biggs. He didn't even know my real first name, he thought it was Calvin. He said I knew he had a gun, which I didn't. He tried to say I orchestrated the whole thing. That I was telling everyone, "You know what your job is," when we were waiting for the delivery man to show up. Which is a lie. Then, he said, I was holding the delivery man from behind, which is true, I was going through his pockets (we found less than four dollars) and later in the statement Martique said I must have done something because the gun "just went off," and he said I took everything and ran.

The next statement came from Shaheed on April 19. The police, at this point, don't know anything except what Martique told them. They came back to Shaheed because he was the one who made the first phone call. He told them he was walking a girl home, heard a shot at the corner, and saw a car with lights. He saw a person riding a bike and a big guy over 6 feet and 200 pounds. He said he started looking for Marty and went to Justin's house where 9 guys were hanging out. He started giving up a lot of things. He told them he saw Marty, Biggs, and Justin. The cops told him: I don't think you're being honest. They came back on April 20 and gave him 8 photos and he pointed me out. So far, they knew the people involved, Biggs, Marty and Steph. Van was the lookout. They didn't wind up getting to him.

The next person they talked to was Justin on April 21st. He was 17

45

years old and the oldest of all of us. He was the guy on the bicycle. They gave him immunity from prosecution, and he became the star witness. Everything he said was then taken as gospel because he was granted immunity. He told them we were playing ball, and we said we needed money, we needed a car. He said Biggs said we should order a pizza and get the man's money and car. Take a joy ride.

So all these people were talking, except me. They didn't have anyone with specific information except Marty who admitted he shot the guy, but who was also saying I was the orchestrator. The only way I knew everyone was talking was that my grandma's friend from the neighborhood told her everything and my grandma confronted me.

That's when my uncle said I needed a lawyer. That was around the 10th or 15th of April. I wasn't arrested until April 26.

On May 28, my lawyer told me that everyone had made statements, and that the prosecution wanted to make a deal. The deal was 12 ½ to 25 years for 3rd Degree Murder in exchange for testimony against Martique. It was a tough deal to take because it ran against all my values. They said I could get life or the death penalty (it turns out the courts had made a new ruling that juveniles couldn't). So either I accept the deal or go to trial. The main witness was Justin, and he could put both me and Martique away forever. With all those fingers pointing at me, I had to take the deal. I made a statement in preparation.

I explained my involvement and I accepted the guilty plea. It hit the newspapers and television: "Teen Guilty. Agrees to Testify." I was featured on all the big news stations and in the press as both the perpetrator and recipient of a great deal for the crime that I was only an accessory to. Martique was hardly mentioned. They grabbed onto the

THE UNSPOKEN TRUTH

fact that I'm a big guy and because the plan was to order food and rob the delivery guy, that I must have been hungry. It was all just absurd.

There are the lessons I learned from all this:

1. Be careful who you call your friends: the code of the street doesn't stand up under pressure.

2. Lies and gossip always follow a crime until the facts about it don't matter anymore.

3. The media doesn't care about what really happened. They only dramatize what will captivate readers/viewers and make their advertisers happy.

4. You can't believe everything you hear. End of story.

Chapter 7

Culture Shock

Since I pleaded guilty in May 2004 there was no trial and I was supposed to be sentenced, but I requested postponement because I wanted to get my diploma, which they granted me.

However, a week and half before I got sentenced, the juvenile block had a riot. Things had escalated on the block, and when school let out, someone punched another guy and everyone else, including me, started fighting. The guards called the response team, the response team swarmed the block and sprayed us all with mace to control us.

Everybody's on the ground, 15 or 20 of us who were identified as the fighters were handcuffed and pepper sprayed. They put you in your cell to clear the area, then they put you in the hole.

The hole is at the back of the block. You're administrated to in the hole, that is, they bring you food trays. You're not allowed out for anything except to shower.

I knew I was going to be sentenced. Much before that I wrote a letter to Judge Benjamin Lerner, in the Philadelphia County Court of Common Pleas, who was the sentencing judge of my case. I wrote him that I was only 15 years old. I asked him to give me a break, give me a chance, due to my lack of knowledge. He responded to me on the day of

THE UNSPOKEN TRUTH

the sentencing, saying, "I appreciated your letter of remorse, but due to the severity of the case," he would have to follow the protocol and sentencing guidelines. Nonetheless, he encouraged me to not give up. Not take this as a last resort. He said, take this opportunity to learn from your mistakes and plan to be somebody.

I was in the hole when I was called out for my sentencing. Then, once I got sentenced, they put me in a cell by myself because I was now property of the state.

A lot of guards, a lot of teachers, a lot of staff, they always looked at me as having potential. I knew the grievance system, how to file a grievance. I was in their favor. Keep your head up, study, get an education, take it. This is not the end of the world, they told me. Everyone was encouraging me, advising me before I went to State. Some of them told me the names of state guards I should look for.

Knowing how things work is power. I always wanted to know how things worked. I wasn't defeated.

It took about a week for the sheriff to pick me up and take me upstate to Graterford Maximum Security Prison.

I was in a bus with others. I was the only juvie. Once you got out of the bus, you went through the metal detector and into a big garage. A 30-foot sliding metal door slammed behind you, a big thick door. Staff was behind computers. I walked down this big long hallway. Strip search in the receiving room, all your clothes go in a box. You're not your own entity anymore. You're a product. Property of the state.

I was still considered a juvenile even though I was in the bus with adults. I was put in a cell by myself.

I am often asked the question: when did you know it was real?

KEENAN HUDSON

This is my answer: When you're going through intake, they ask you a series of questions and the last one is the one that kicks you in the gut. "If something should happen to you in here, where do you want the body sent."

To call it culture shock is an understatement. Jail is an entirely different world. Just to give you an overview: People on the outside believe that the inmates are reforming themselves now that they're locked up, but nothing could be further from the truth. You can get anything in jail that you want—family members, drones, guards bring in drugs (lieutenants, captains, majors: there are lots of corrupt ones).

The guards administer their own kind of justice. Guards try to punish you by not feeding you. If you argue and words are exchanged, things escalate. Weapons get planted in your cell.

There are lots of professionals—doctors, lawyers, businessmen—in the jail, too. By that, I mean guys who know how to do things. Make fixtures out of exit lights. Make knives out of toothbrushes with razors. Guys would put the lock from their cabinet in a sock to hit the guards. Lock in a sock, they call it. Although lock in a sock is pretty low tech, the point is you make do with what you have.

So, there I was at 16. At first, I didn't get how serious it was. I was mentally still a kid. But a life was taken. That's as serious as it gets.

After intake, I went straight to the hole—I was still a juvenile—L-block hole right across from death row. I was there for 30 days. They'd extended my hole time from county because I was in the riot. I was in the hole till they sent me to the classification jail, Camp Hill.

Things were on another level at Graterford. We were on the gate playing Jeopardy, bingo, and family feud, even the food was different,

THE UNSPOKEN TRUTH

pancakes, what meal do you want? Old heads served the young bulls, but you learned don't accept no favors from anybody 'cause they're gonna want a favor in return. You hear a lot of stories. Some guys down there were from the Camp Hill riot in '89. Some went crazy, some sharpen up, send you over Playboy mags, smut magazines.

In Jeopardy, you read the question, for example: in 2004 who was the president of the United States. They call a cell number, say, Cell 42. You answer the question, President Bush. If you win, you get two Nutty Bars, Swiss Rolls, Honey Buns.

The colors in Graterford were: Blues (not classified yet), Browns (population), Orange (hole),

After 30 days in the hole, I was transferred to Camp Hill to get classified. They give you the same tests you got on day one to see if you're lying. They evaluate your mental ability, skill sets, where you were education-wise, psychology.

In Camp Hill, I was in blue, among the adult population. I was there for three months, until they were able to verify my diploma. In the meantime, I had to go to school and wait to be classified.

They have their own reasons for sending you to different places. Parole board is looking for consistency, to see if you have any kind of growth over the years.

After three months there, I was sent to Pine Grove, half adult, half juvenile. I was in the population, including boot camp LVP (leadership development program), but I was only there for six months. Marty was already there. Plus his twin brothers, Kareem and Kayree, were in Pine Grove for totally different crimes. When I got there Marty was in the hole. The court order followed up (the county followed to the state) that Marty

KEENAN HUDSON

and me be separated, so I ended up getting transferred.

While I was there, though, I graduated the boot camp. I was a high honor boot camp graduate. A lot of things I accomplished there in that little bit of time.

Eventually I was transferred, sent to SCI Retreat. It was all adults. By this time I was 17. Legally, they couldn't cell me up with another adult till I was 18. I was population but I was a single cell.

I had a neighbor, next cell, we used to converse through the radiator vent. His name was Chief. He was an Indian, down for about 30-35 years for murder. Sometimes he would bang on the wall because I had the TV blaring or I was yelling out the gate.

I would learn things from Chief. One story that stuck with me. Something happened to him at the poker table. I'm a little upset, he confided to me. What happened, Chief? I asked. I was at the poker table and some guys added some chips. Black guy brought some extra chips. "Tried to rob the pot. I hate to say the word," he said, "it was some slimy nigger shit." Chief felt real comfortable with me even though he was triple my age.

In Retreat, I started working out, getting in shape, playing every sport. I was still searching for me, trying to figure me out, going to the library. I believed there was greatness in me.

I was in Retreat from 2006 till 2010. I was heavily influenced by some top dogs—Chuckie Africa and Shareef aka Reef Man. Most people knew me on the basketball court as Big Baby. I had to work hard to get my game up because I was still a kid. I played amongst some of the top ballers. Just to name a few—Art, 6'9," JT, Dunk, Sheed, and a host of others.

THE UNSPOKEN TRUTH

After that I was transferred out of state to Green Rock Correctional in Virginia.

It was different there. In Pennsylvania, you had a lot redneck guards. In Virginia, a lot of the guards were African-Americans. The hospitality was southern. They spoke to you differently. The way they ran things, though was garbage. It was too locked down. However, I earned different vocationals: computer aided stuff, custodial maintenance (wax and floor specialist). I had a block store and was a general on B-block. Green Rock was a place where I experienced something that would change my life forever (keep reading to find out). Pennsylvania had already shaped us to respect the guards. You got 30 days in the hole if you disrespected a guard. If we disrespected a guard in Virginia you got 7 days in the hole.

After 2012 I was sent back to Retreat. If you come back and you don't have any infractions, you can transfer anywhere you want to.

I was there for 8 months. Then I went to Albion, in Erie, Pennsylvania.

Albion was a wild jail. A lot of violence, a lot of gay activity. One of the inmates got killed when I was there. Lots of guards getting beat up, stabbed up, a hit list out for guards. Many inmates got killed there. A guard getting beat up almost every other week. Lots of gangs. If the head gang honcho said you had to do something, you better do it or they would come for you. I saw more violence there than anywhere else.

I was in Albion from 2013 till 2016.

Life in prison has its own rules and the rules are pretty much the same everywhere. It even has its own form of currency. If you were lucky, you got money put on your books to buy stuff off commissary. You got

KEENAN HUDSON

paid on the books by taking block worker jobs. But otherwise, you had to trade your talents to get the jailhouse currency, which is, believe it or not, soups and kites. Kites are like buckhorns, like a homemade rolled cigarette. By giving your phone time to someone, 15-minute time slots, once a day, 5 dollars to accept a call, then $2.60 a minute. Not everyone in prison is illiterate, but I would get 5 soups for writing a letter home for somebody or filling out commissary sheets.

Mostly, though, prison is boring. Typical day, things are highly predictable. At 5:30 AM, we have standing count with lights on. Guard passes by, you can go back to sleep. Nobody goes out till count clears 30 minutes later. The officers will announce it on loud speakers, kitchen workers are called out.

When they start doing big line movement, when a mass of the population is about to come out, they do it slowly. If something were to happen the inmates have total control. We always outnumber the guards.

At 6:30 AM, everyone goes to breakfast. Your morning meal, prison portions are controlled—hot or cold cereal, 2% milk, fruit, 2 boiled eggs, pancakes, French toast or waffles. Then you return to the block.

They call work lines at 8 AM. School lines are called at 8:15. You go where you're supposed to go.

At 8:30 AM you have morning yard. You can exercise, play handball, horseshoes, bocce ball, soccer, football, volleyball. They have picnic tables out there and you can play cards, dominoes, chess, checkers. You stay in the yard till the bell rings at 9:15 (halftime), then you go back to your cell.

During those times there are call outs—medical appointments,

THE UNSPOKEN TRUTH

sick call, dentist appointments, commissary, a call out for a checkup, you pick up things from the property, church, work outs, cross-fit training.

At 10 AM, you go back to the block and everyone is in lockdown until lunch.

Everyone waits for chow. Chow begins around 11:30. Everyone goes to chow. Depending on how big the jail is—1,200 inmates, some have 4,000—it ends around 12:30, 12:35. Immediately after chow, back in the cell, another count. Count ends around 1:00.

Same process happens again. At 1:15, yard is called again. You're there until 3 o'clock. You go in the yard or stay in your cell. That ends at 3:45 or 4:00. Throughout the day you can sign up for the phone or take showers.

There were CI (Correctional Industries) jobs, hard-to-get-into jobs: shoe shop, laundry, manufacturing of t-shirts, of inmate uniforms. They paid from 150 to 200 dollars a month. The lesser jobs paid 19 cents an hour—kitchen, machine shop, electric shop, plumbing shop, paint shop. Prison has departments for everything. Some people get apprenticeships like in the culinary arts. I did.

Aunt Brenda and Mom-Mom with me when I received my culinary arts diploma.

KEENAN HUDSON

When they call out for one of them, you get your pass and go to your job.

At 6:00 PM, it's yard again or gym. At that time, you have passes from a lot of volunteers—Bible studies, college classes, music people come in to teach music classes. You're out from 6 to 8:45 PM when there's another countdown for the rest of the night.

There is an honor block (good behavior). I wasn't on the honor block till I was about to come home, when I came up to see parole. I had to go to the honor block to make cell space for others coming in. I thought it was overrated. It wasn't my vibe.

Here's one thing about prison. You always have to be on your guard. You never want to feel content. For example, never wear shower shoes on the block. You think nothing will happen to you. But anyone is liable to jump off, like if somebody violated the code. You always have to be on alert. Because of the size of the jail, as soon as there is a fight, all movement stops. Like I said, there are more of us than there are guards, so as soon as something gets out of control, everyone has to lock down.

In your cell it's possible to have some amenities. You can buy a TV, you can buy cable, you can buy a radio, a nightlight. You have one cell mate unless you're a short timer, then you live in a dorm. Guys who are doing major time have single cells (Z-code). Rapists always have single cells.

So you get into a rhythm, a routine. But you never really get used to it, and it's not home.

Chapter 8

Becoming a Man in Prison

The world as I knew it stopped when the gate locked behind me in Graterford. I went in as a 15-year-old kid, and that world ended that day. It was like the old me was frozen in time and I had to learn everything from scratch. It wasn't just technology, although that was a big thing. It was more that I had to learn to be a man in there. Before she passed, my mom said, "Keenan, I can do a lot for you, but I can't teach you to be a man." On her deathbed, my mom told my cousin Jennifer that she wasn't worried about my sister and my older brother, but she was worried about me, what would happen to me. She knew how people were towards me, because I was always into something.

And that was on the outside. Becoming a man in prison is harder because there are fewer role models to choose from. Lots of the lessons I learned were from just watching. Some of the lessons I learned were by someone putting me in my place. I was a child, mentally and physically, but the average age was about 40. I already told you how I learned in county jail to not taunt the older guys when the guard dragged me over to the cell where the old head was. That's not a lesson you ever forget. You never know who you're dealing with.

And you never trust anyone. You can be buddies with someone

KEENAN HUDSON

one day, the next day they're jumping you. It's tough, but you learn to deal.

One of the things about prison is that you remember faces. You're around people so much, and if I'm around you all the time, I'll remember you. If you go to a new environment and you see a face, it's like a snapshot. Ah, yeah, I remember that guy. That's why some guards get scared (typically, there are 20 inmates to every guard), they know we remember.

One of my mentors was Chuckie Africa. He was probably the most influential man in there. He taught me about music but also about knowledge and power.

These are the lessons I learned during my incarceration.

Lesson #1: Never let your mind wander

Always stay involved. Knowledge is power. Learn as much as possible. I would go to the library and read Entrepreneur, Forbes, Black Enterprise. I never stayed complacent. I stayed active as much as possible.

A mind wandering on its own, especially an uneducated mind, is a mind that is headed for madness, depression, or trouble. I was never idle on the outside. I always had something going on so it was easier for me than for some guys to keep myself occupied. Even though my body was captured, I never allowed my mind to be idle, and I made sure my body stayed as active as possible. I played all the sports I could—played basketball, worked out in the gym lifting weights. Now that I was off the Ritalin, I found I could more easily control my weight. That, and working

58

THE UNSPOKEN TRUTH

out, and the prison controlled portions in the chow hall, made it easier for me, and I learned how it felt to be in good shape, probably the best shape I've been in my life.

I signed up for every activity I could—culinary arts, plumbing. college classes. In addition, the judge required that you take certain programs. An inmate got out and killed a state trooper in Jersey, so they changed the rules about what's required. Now you have to take Violence Prevention, Victim Awareness, SOP (sex offender program.)

Lesson #2: Mind Your Own Business

Just because you have an opinion about something or someone doesn't mean you have to share it. In fact, sharing your opinion usually leads to confrontation and in prison that leads to violence.

Sex offenders get no peace in prison. The guards call them out. They make sure everyone knows what they did.

There was an incident that really sticks out in my mind. What happened was, I was locked in the juvenile cells and the adults brought us food. We started making fun of our server saying, "Look at the faggot." Never fight with a homosexual. The majority of them know how to box and they will humiliate you.

So, when I say "Mind your own business," I also mean never taunt someone you don't know or someone you think can't get to you.

As a side note to this point about homosexuals: if you argue or fight with a homosexual, everyone is going to assume you're one too or in a relationship with one. Otherwise, why would you even pay attention?

People respected me because I ran in my own lane. I was laid

59

KEENAN HUDSON

back and humble, no drama. Yeah, I got write-ups for arguing with a guard, but I never antagonized fellow inmates. If I got into arguments, it never escalated. Lots of the inmates were gang members. Vice Lords. Latin Kings. Bloods. I remained neutral, even though people think I'm a Blood because they're my homies. But I kept in my lane, minded my own business. When you're associated with a gang, you take on all of their business. If you get into a fight with a gang member, like in a poker game or a basketball game, your entire gang has to come to your defense. If a gang member snitched on somebody, you have to air him out, stab him, shank him, bang him out. Lots of New York terms. You got to jump him. All the gang members answer to the OG, original gangster. He's the top dog of whoever's there.

Lesson #3: Surround Yourself with Winners

Most people think that in prison there are nothing but cold-blooded murderers and thieves. There were actually a lot of professionals in prison as well—ex-judges who lied under oath, ex-lawyers, ex-sports figures, dirty cops and guards who slept with female inmates. These were all high-profile people. Guys in federal prison are at the top of their game. They're real sharp. They're there because they made mistakes.

My greatest passion was getting to people who were at the top of their game. These were the people I hung with. Some of my peers had the same mindset, but they were getting out sooner than me. I had a long sentence, but still, we would brainstorm things that we wanted to do when we got out.

There's no question in my mind that if I hadn't been hanging with

THE UNSPOKEN TRUTH

my co-defendants, I wouldn't have been involved in the crime. The only reason I went along with them was because of peer pressure.

You can succumb to the pressure of loser peers or winner peers. Pick the winners.

Once I was in prison and got my footing, I knew I had to change my mindset. I started taking college courses. I realized that most of the inmates were close to illiterate, but I was so interested in everything I could learn, already trying to plan for what I was going to do when I got out, and because I was so interested, the professors took an interest in me. Most of them couldn't understand what I was doing there. That's one of the reasons I wrote *The Incarceration of the Juvenile Mind* while I was there—to help people understand how people who weren't necessarily bad could be persuaded by peer pressure to do bad things, especially young people.

I started reading lots of books from the prison library: Martin Luther King, Jr., Malcom X, Nelson Mandela. They were all incarcerated and used that time to think and plan what they would do when they were released. Since I was associating with people like them, even if only through their writing, I was already starting to surround myself with winners.

I believe that these three tenets: Don't let your mind wander, Mind your own Business, Surround yourself with Winners, helped me grow up and into a man while serving my time. These three tenets are also the basis of my organization, Kingdom Humility, which seeks to serve a diverse community of people by providing life skill solutions for individuals seeking mentorship, encouragement, musical education, and motivational speaking. It gave me the discipline to create City Rental Cars,

KEENAN HUDSON

Hope Real Estate, and Reform Financial Group.

But these tenets weren't the only things that helped form me while I was serving time. I also had access to musical knowledge and business knowledge, which I took full advantage of and which are serving me now. I'll talk about those next.

Chapter 9

The Business of Education and Business

I already told you that I postponed my sentencing so I could get my high school diploma. I was definitely driven to learn as much as I could about as many subjects as I could. I read about MLK, Nelson Mandela, Malcolm X. Hearing about these people, people who made a big impact when they got out of prison, inspired me. I knew I should get as much education as possible, and that is one thing that prison does provide. I always knew I wanted to be something BIG. I would study a pocket dictionary, a word a day.

During the time I was in the county jail, Hildebrand Pilzer III, the principal I told you about who turned everything around in there, got a couple of us together to write a book, *Broken Promises*. I was only 15 or 16 at that time. He was a huge influence on me. He agreed with me that I was going to be something big.

My favorite professor by far, though, was Professor Michael McGaw, who taught business and computer in education classes. None of the other professors really understood us like Professor McGaw, and he taught me as much as I was willing to learn. He was the epitome of what I desired to be, in other words, the best.

It was always a zeal I had in me, to create something big. I had a big imagination. There's no imagination involved in smart phones. They

KEENAN HUDSON

do all the creating for you. And then I met Professor McGaw.

I was actively in the culinary arts program when I connected with him. He was a business educator, basic and advanced. How to be money smart. So, after I heard about him, I signed up for Basic Business Education. There were 15 in the class. He made us learn to type on the computer. We had to learn the keyboard for a whole month. After typing, he taught us Word and Excel. In Excel, he taught us how to do formulas and spreadsheets which I use today.

Those were the only two applications he was supposed to train us on, but he took it to another level. I could do fonts, line it up. I could reproduce everything, headers, footers. He always gave us pop quizzes. He always expected high quality work. He expected people to advance. One time I overheard a student complaining to him that he was doing the best he could and McGaw responded, "Your best is not good enough. If this is not for you, go find something else." Most of us loved him because he knew his stuff. I always remember what Professor McGaw said, "I expect people to advance." What a great attitude.

He told us he didn't pay a dime for college. He dug up every grant he could get his hands on. That introduced me to the concept of OPM (other people's money).

He told us that there are three ways to control people: Money, Politics, and Fear (violence). Even the guards came in and asked his advice about investments. I made notes about that. He was at the top.

I got the idea that I could be a businessman like Jay-Z. He has lots of businesses. He has an airline service, which is the Uber of the air for rich people. That's the mindset I like to be around. Creating some kind of generational wealth. My long range plan is to create big apartment-living

THE UNSPOKEN TRUTH

and hotel-type complexes.

A lot of people aren't meant to be with you forever. Some are meant to be with you a moment or a season. Some forever, yes. Professor McGaw is one of the people whose influence is with me forever.

Although I realized that there was no reason for me to get a college degree once I was released, I attended Lehigh-Carbon County Community college while I was in prison. They came into the prison, and I obtained 15 credits.

I am still learning. The only TV I watch is documentaries: Pablo Escobar, Nicki Barnes, Alpo, Azie, Rich Porter, Frank Lucas, El Chapo. Real life, Real people. I want to learn how they established their enterprises. I was attracted to their mindset of orchestration. I admire it, while not condoning the activities they were involved in.

Even now, I push myself to learn as much as I can. Break the bid up. You don't just do one thing—play ball, go to church, talent shows. I just knew, even then, I was going to be great. If I have to have solitude to develop my message, I will forego the ladies and hanging out. I've been out five years now. Just being out five years is an accomplishment.

I applaud people who are at the top of their game. I want to learn from that person. Knowledge is power.

There's a saying, "You want to hide something from a black person, put it in a book." I want to be the opposite. You can't hide knowledge from me. There is no stopping a person with knowledge.

65

Chapter 10

Learning Music and Finding God

I was always the person that teachers picked out as having potential, and I was able to concentrate on learning things while I was in prison. I had a few mentors in prison, and I can't stress enough how important it is to have someone believe that you have potential. And everything I learned while in prison I used later.

A good thing about the prison system, in Pennsylvania at least, is that you don't necessarily have to spend your entire sentence in one place. While I was in SCI Retreat, we were informed that Pennsylvania prisons were overcrowded, and so Pennsylvania signed an agreement with Michigan and Virginia to house the overflow. There are 28 prisons in Pennsylvania. The prisoners from the 14 jails in the eastern part of the state were to go to Virginia. The prisoners from the 14 jails in the western part of the state were to go to Michigan.

You could apply for the transfer, so I did. Me and my cellie, Miles 'Marcy' Clinkscales, wanted a change of scenery so we signed up. But enough men weren't signing up, so the state started selecting men. Some didn't even know they were on a list. Those who were selected for a transfer had their heads and beards shaved off, even the men who kept beards for religious reasons. In Pennsylvania, you don't need a hair exemption, but in Virginia you do. You were basically stripped of all your

66

THE UNSPOKEN TRUTH

rights when you transferred, but you didn't know when you were going until the night before when they came to your cell with a meal and said, "Pack up. You're leaving." They gave you a meal because you were going to be on the road for a long way with no stops for meals. However, none of the prisoners would eat the meals because they knew that they'd be on the road for more than six hours with maybe one stop. If you shit or pissed yourself, that was your problem. The guards didn't care.

So, I was packed up to go to Virginia. We didn't go in the regular prison buses, like they used in Pennsylvania. We were shipped in what they called submarine buses—40 prisoners in a bus, 10 buses in the fleet. They chained our feet and waist and handcuffed us with one hand over the other, all secured with a lockbox to keep it together. They blocked the roads we were on and cops had M-16 rifles out. We left from Camp Hill, a classification prison, where they gave us another meal that no one ate. But the justice system is clear: they have to feed you. Everyone threw their meal in the trash. There was no food on the bus. The trip was 8 hours because we stopped halfway for a one-hour bathroom break. You can imagine how long it took to get 10 busloads of shackled men in and out of the bus and in and out of the bathroom.

When we finally got to Virginia, it was like a different world. The guards, the staff, the medical personnel, were all greeting us. The medical personnel came on the buses before we unloaded to take our blood pressures and temperature because it was so hot. Virginia is a southern state and the difference in hospitality between Virginia and Pennsylvania is huge. They were very friendly. We were like, "What the hell?" We thought it was a setup. Nothing like Pennsylvania. The mentality was way different. Pennsylvania was so strict because of all the prison riots years

67

KEENAN HUDSON

before. The guards would poke you to establish their authority. That's part of their tactic to assert control. It's mostly like when you're transferring, like in Camp Hill. The reality is that your home jail is not as bad. But they still don't give a shit about you.

After we unloaded, they herded us into a gymnasium. They had stations there, like a maze, chaplain, nurse. You could sign up for stuff. It was a big intake. They took the cuffs off. We were strip searched. First time Virginia had ever been through something like this.

After the intake, we were assigned to the cafeteria, where we had a meal. The food was way better than the feed in Pennsylvania. What the hell? The day we came down there, they gave us double portions. It was so good and different, everybody ate everything. After that meal, the portions were controlled, but it was still good. It beat Pennsylvania.

After intake and our meal, they sent us to our housing unit. It was a new environment. A lot of the guards, I'd say 95%, were African-American, but you still had white guards. But we still didn't trust it. There were things that weren't so great, though, like we couldn't have more than one pair of sneakers, so we couldn't play basketball. That was upsetting.

Also, in Pennsylvania, you had control of your lights, on or off. The only time you didn't was when you were in the hole. In the hole in PA, even when lights are off you had an emergency light. In Virginia, the emergency lights were on all night. It's state of the art, they said, but there was a lot of sleep deprivation. It was a different environment.

The lifers were happy they had a change of scenery, any kind: ice machine, microwave. You get it. It was a brand new chapter. You don't know what was going to happen.

THE UNSPOKEN TRUTH

Another difference was that if you didn't have a job, they didn't support you the way Pennsylvania did. Think of society: You don't have a job, you can file for unemployment, welfare. In prison if you don't have a job, you sign up for GLP, General Labor Pool. Virginia didn't do that. If you didn't have money, you couldn't go to commissary. A lot of people were angry about that. They had time in, and a lot of them didn't have any more family to send them money, including me. 90% of the jail weren't going home. I had a lot of people on my block from SCI Dallas, and I'd say about 90% were lifers.

This Virginia prison is called Green Rock Correctional Center. I was forced to get a job on the block. I tried to find a job right away, but it was hard. They didn't have job openings. They were creating jobs. They had to 'cause if we didn't have anything to keep us busy we would rebel.

My homie, Miles 'Marcy' Clinkscales, is one of the smartest individuals in the country.

My homie, Tyrone 'T.Y.' Kemp, is one of the best boxers to come out of Philadelphia. We've known each other since George Washington High School.

KEENAN HUDSON

Eventually, I ended up getting a block job. By this time, I had 8 years in, and I was still being me. I still didn't trust many people. Homies I thought I could trust, they would talk trash behind my back. I started sending requests for getting a job, get some education. It wasn't as fast a process as it was in PA. I had to figure things out for myself, So when I couldn't get a job, finally, my entrepreneur sense kicked in. I saw there were a lot of coffee drinkers. A lot of the old guys drink coffee all day if they can. I started to buy bags of coffee off the cafeteria, and I would sell shots of coffee. Out of one bag, which cost 3 dollars, I would divide the bag up and sell shots for 50 cents apiece. I was getting about 25 shots out of a bag, 4 times my money. I opened up my own Starbucks. I sold soups— I give you 2, next week you pay me back with 4, it was profitable. It was illegal activity, of course, but they turned a blind eye.

I was on a block. The time structure was totally different. You couldn't navigate the way you could in PA. The first thing I did there was get right with the principal of the school, Jeffry Milner, and I took CAD (Computer Aided Design) classes. Then a job opened up for block custodian, and I jumped into custodial maintenance. At first, I started out by cleaning the showers and wiping things down. Eventually, I learned how to strip and wax vinyl floors. Virginia took a lot of pride in their floors, their vinyl floors look like marble. I am probably the best floor cleaner and polisher out there.

As a block worker, I could do what I wanted. I had favor amongst the guards. A lot of people in the block looked up to me. I was only 20-21, but I always had influence over people. If there was an issue with something, people would come to me to make sure it got straightened out. I didn't play games. I gave straight answers.

THE UNSPOKEN TRUTH

Me at the top level of stripping and waxing floors.

By the time I was able to get a block worker job, they opened up a lot of jobs. They saw that people needed jobs to survive.

Around this time, I met a woman, Minister Sonya Jennings, who was a prison guard. She was a church-going lady. She loved the Lord, loved God. She was very kind. Everyone loved her. She used to say, "Keenan, I see some potential in you." She persuaded me to start going to church services. I started reading the Bible, which I found to be full of life lessons and experiences. So, I got a relationship with God in prison. I dabbled in it when I was a kid, but I was now ready to hear the message and I feel blessed with the gifts that were given to me and are still being given to me.

There was something about Miss Jennings' glow, the spirit of God upon her. Every day she worked, she would pour into me something uplifting. She said, "Keenan, I don't know what it is, but you have potential to do something out of here. This place is not for you."

For two years straight, Miss Jennings was pouring uplifting messages into me. I started developing my faith. People prayed over me.

KEENAN HUDSON

It kept me humble, it kept me balanced, and prepared me to go for the next level. I realized then that whatever I put into the universe, I get back. You reap what you sow. Since then, I've done a lot of giving. I've been blessed with so much. I think that one idea—that whatever you do to the least to my creatures, you do to God—if everyone thought it even once a day it would make the world a whole lot better. I always say, Christians, can you walk the walk? Or are you all talk? I'm all about action. I know with my faith in God and his favor upon my life, I will accomplish what I want.

At that time, though, I was just learning and so I was just going as a participant. Going to some of the bible studies.

So here I was, getting my skills up. For two years straight, I was with a bunch of lifers. I gravitated to some of them that had huge names, influential prisoners. Smiley Akbar (Fruit of Islam) from Norris Street. He had a life sentence. He was knowledgeable about a lot of things, even though we didn't have the same beliefs. Once, I was a little agitated about something—someone said something that set me off. He said to me, "Brother Biggs, I know you are frustrated about something, but you never want to show your emotions in prison. That person now knows how to get to you."

Over time, I would grow more and more in Virginia.

They did have track and basketball, and I would volunteer to set up the equipment. I was on the call-out for that. We were able to start a basketball league. I was still in top shape.

This is how we were able to do it: When we got accustomed to the prison, we started hiding sneakers so we could play. The basketball league was catching the flow the last six months we were there. It was deep. So, we created the basketball league. We ran a championship. It was a stamp. The people we were around, we may not see those people anymore when we leave VA. We may never see them again as long as we live.

In prison we take sports very seriously. I didn't have a childhood. I only saw sports on TV, so the pictures I took there are memorabilia.

Above, SCI Retreat Champs, in browns (me the only one cracking a smile). Below, me in top shape, in brown.

Virginia Department of Corrections Champs, in blues

After two years, Pennsylvania terminated the contract with Virginia, and we heard that we had to go back to PA. A lot of the lifers were hurt because of this. Right about then, though, the chaplain in Green Rock was forming a revival. Even though I was going over to the church, I still didn't know who God was. I still wasn't living like no Christian. I didn't know what that was.

They were going to have different churches come in every day. Miss Jennings church came in on a Friday, and she was preaching. The church that came in was The Ramp Church International under Bishop S. Y. Younger and music minister Bruce Johnson. It was amazing. Some musicians were there. They tore the place up. Pastors were praying over me and prophesizing that I would be a musician. They told me, if you're going to learn music, learn the theory. They explained the difference and the importance of learning theory instead of playing by ear, because

THE UNSPOKEN TRUTH

where the money is you've got to know theory.

When I came back after the revival, after the prophecy, I welcomed the Lord and Savior into my life and my whole life changed. The scales dropped from my eyes. I became a different person. I looked at the world differently. I was filled with the Holy Spirit.

The prophecy of me becoming a musician stuck with me. In the Virginia prison, you weren't allowed to have instruments in the cells, so I took out every music book in the library and I read them all. I learned my scales. There wasn't much else I could learn there, so I was glad that we were going back to Pennsylvania.

I still had another four years to go. I was sent back to SCI Retreat and after eight months I put in for a transfer. During that eight months I was able to get back into advanced computing with Professor McGaw. He was asking for me. There were some things he wanted to complete with me. In Retreat during this time, I got with Chuckie Africa. He knew his music theory and I learned a lot from him. More than that, he was politically inspiring and raised my consciousness. We got closer because he knew a lot of music. We would meet in the yard and jam with other musicians.

I put in to transfer to three jails: Rockview, Crescent, and Albion. They told me to pack my stuff, I was going to SCI Dallas (State Correctional Institution in Dallas, PA). I put Dallas on all my stuff. The day that I went to the hub in Smithfield, they said, "Hudson, you're going to Albion." There was a big mix-up with my property, but I was on the bus to Albion. On the bus to Albion it was so cold I was shaking. But one of the reasons I wanted to transfer was to work on my music, so I had to keep that in my mindset.

KEENAN HUDSON

Albion was tough. As explained in the previous chapters, there was a lot of violence in Albion. I was in the middle of some stuff, little riots, guys getting stabbed, getting their heads cracked, but usually I stayed in my lane. I knew the Bloods and the Latin Kings, but I kept neutral. They respected me, came to me for advice, some things they wanted me to research, some of them came for the music.

My big outlet was going to chapel and playing music there. I was hired to work in the chapel as a music person. The thing is there's a lot of jealousy in music. So, here I was this guy who knew everything about theory, but rhythm was a different matter. There was a Puerto Rican guy, Barbosa, in the Spanish church who asked me to come and play, they didn't have a musician. But when I started playing, it became obvious that I didn't know Spanish rhythm, so people started throwing me down. I started listening to tapes to get a Latin rhythm, and pretty soon I got it,

During my time there, 90% of my time was spent in the chapel. Even though there were a lot of ups and downs I was able to learn from good mentors. Just to name a few—Big Jungle (Ramsey Wood), Shelby Zablotny, Jerry Rouser, Bronco. I was still learning my craft. During that time, there were three different service—Protestant, Spanish, and Catholic. I was still learning to play. There were other musicians there—a lot of jealousy and envy, they didn't want to give up their spot, they wanted to do things their way. The Spanish church reached out—if you could come help us out, we would appreciate it. I was getting used to the Latin rhythm. The only reason I got better at piano in general was because I started playing over there at the Spanish church. I was mostly in the choir. The music director didn't want me to play because he didn't want the competition, at least, that's what I felt at the time. Little did I know,

76

THE UNSPOKEN TRUTH

it was a growing process, a learning process. All the performance skills I learned were from the Spanish church. I did almost three years down there. The first two years were rough, but I learned a lot about music, being both a performer and a teacher. During that time, I would play now and then at regular services, but not so much. I practiced in my cell, had jam sessions in the yard with other musicians. Jimmy Dale Morris (Apostolic Faith) hired me for the chapel to be a musician. I was in charge of the Spanish choir and the Protestant choir.

During my stay at Albion, I was still learning, despite there being a lot of verbal disputes. A lot more headaches building up on each other. Long story short—I eventually started gaining favor with other inmates and the guards. The warden had actually asked me to teach at the SNU (Special Needs Unit) and SMU (Special Mental Unit) for people who had mental health conditions. That's when I realized I could teach. I started teaching people music in the Spanish choir and the Protestant choir. It was my calling to help people learn.

I was off the block most of the time, but still I saw a lot of stabbings. People getting their heads cracked.

My musical journey was escalating. I wasn't the best, but I knew what I was capable of.

I grew shoulder to shoulder in my faith. One group made a big impact on me—a Bible study, Life in the Holy Spirit, came in. They specialized in teaching the gifts of the Holy Spirit. These people blessed my life. They came in once a week, Tuesday nights. The most important to me were a married couple, Dan and Irene, and Denise. They were the ones who really helped me. They taught a lot of principles of the Bible, and how to utilize the gifts of the spirit in daily living. They had a huge

77

KEENAN HUDSON

impact on my life as a spiritual person. Every night at Albion they had something different and I took advantage of everything.

I knew my time was coming to an end. I had to stop playing basketball because things can get really heated, and when people know you're going home, they'll play on that. I had to keep a low profile, stay focused until it was time to get released. I had to move to the honor block, so everyone knew I was going home soon, everyone knew you saw the parole board within a year.

Then, the last year was my parole year.

Chapter 11

A Parole Plan in Hand

Parole is tough. You have to go in front of a parole board of 8 people including professionals like an ex-DA, lawyers, ex-judges. These are the type of people that are on the board. If they approve of your parole, they give you a list of conditions of your parole, which you include in your re-entry plan.

I made up my own re-entry plan which included lists of all my educational and academic credentials, all of my vital records, my re-entry and parole plan highlights, letters of recommendation and support, and my religious credentials. It's helpful to have all this in one place so you can promote yourself when you get out. Also, so you realize in a concrete way all that you accomplished while you were incarcerated.

One of the letters of recommendation I got was from my sentencing judge, Judge Benjamin Lerner, who was now serving in the mayor of Philadelphia's cabinet. Everything I remembered that he told me played a big part in my re-entry plan. He was a colleague of my attorney, Mr. Rose, and he remembered me and wrote a letter for me. In my re-entry plan, I laid out all the key points of what I was going to do. It was about 40 pages and included things like—having escape plans if support system fails, closest shelter.

79

KEENAN HUDSON

Everything is going to last for a moment. No one is going to carry you. Key point—Anybody can get put on their feet but not everybody can stay on their feet. Can you swim in the deep end? You have to learn to swim. I have written a book, *The Re-Entry Guide*, which explains the whole process of re-entering, so I won't go into detail here. But having a well thought out plan builds confidence. You can see all that you have done with your time and who your supporters are. It will also help you build your Home Plan and Employment Plan, which you will need.

But no matter how much you have in these categories, and I had a lot, I believe that the most important thing to try to get together before you're released is your head. I lost a lot of life in prison. Almost fifteen years. As important as your resumé and physical plans are, it's even more important to try to calibrate what that loss of life means to your future.

I trusted God through the whole process. After I was interviewed by the parole board, I waited four weeks for the decision. That was an anxious time, because everything was coming on so fast. I was already working outside the prison, so I saw the changed landscape and saw all the new cars. Each morning, I wondered if today would be the day when I would get the decision, my green sheet. When it was time to pick up your green sheet you were on a call-out. There's a piece of paper on the block, a call-out list, and if you're listed for a green sheet, you get a pass to go over to the Administration Office.

So, everybody knew I was getting my green sheet, but nobody knew what the result was. When I went to see the parole agent, she said, "Yeah, you got parole." When I went back to the block, I was acting sad so nobody would ask me. By this time there was a new chaplain, Reverend Scott Graubar, a very knowledgeable and educated guy, both

THE UNSPOKEN TRUTH

biblically and secularly. He was a very on-time and a very great teacher. I learned from him just as much as he learned from the foreign environment he was working in. He had a lot of influence over me from his experience of life. I sat under and gained what he had to offer from the bickering and ups and downs in the chapel, I told the chaplain, and he congratulated me. I tried to keep it a secret, but pretty soon everyone knew.

BURTON A. ROSE
ATTORNEY AT LAW

1731 SPRING GARDEN STREET
PHILADELPHIA, PA 19130-3893
OFFICE (215) 564-5550
FAX (215) 567-6809
EMAIL: barose@baroselaw.com

March 21, 2016

Pennsylvania Board of Probation and Parole
1101 S. Front Street
Harrisburg, PA 17104

RE: Keenan Hudson
Date of Birth: January 16, 1989
#GL-0270 – SCI Albion

Dear Sir or Madam:

Please be advised that I am the attorney for the above named inmate whose case is to be considered for parole this year.

On September 7, 2004, Keenan Hudson pleaded guilty to charges of Murder of the Third Degree and Criminal Conspiracy as part of a negotiated plea bargain. On November 28, 2005, Judge Benjamin Lerner of the Philadelphia Court of Common Pleas sentenced the Defendant to a term of not less than 12 ½ nor more than 25 years imprisonment, with credit for time served since April 26, 2004 (when the Defendant self-surrendered to the police). There was no appeal or further litigation challenging the conviction or sentence.

I have had the opportunity to review reference letters submitted on behalf of Mr. Hudson from the Chaplain at SCI Albion as well as from the Pastor of Oasis City Church in Philadelphia. I have spoken with Mr. Hudson. I am familiar with the Certificates that he has earned as a result of participation in many educational and behavioral programs at the Institution. Based upon my understanding of Mr. Hudson's adjustment since incarceration, it would appear that he has made an outstanding effort towards reform and rehabilitation.

I also note that Mr. Hudson has written a letter to the family of the victim in which he has expressed remorse for his role in the homicide which resulted in his present incarceration. He has become a very religious man and I am confident that he has learned a terrible lesson that he will not forget when he is finally released.

KEENAN HUDSON

Pennsylvania Board of Probation and Parole
March 21, 2016
Page 2

I hope that the Parole Board will see that Keenan Hudson has really had a true life transformation in prison. I request that he be paroled at the earliest opportunity.

Thank you for your consideration.

Respectfully submitted,

BURTON A. ROSE
Attorney for Defendant

BAR/cab
cc: Keenan Hudson

FIRST JUDICIAL DISTRICT OF PENNSYLVANIA
COURT OF COMMON PLEAS
JUDICIAL CHAMBERS

BENJAMIN LERNER
SENIOR JUDGE

March 7, 2016

THE JUSTICE JUANITA KIDD STOUT CENTER
FOR CRIMINAL JUSTICE
1301 FILBERT STREET, SUITE 1220
PHILADELPHIA, PA 19107
(215) 683-7077/78

Keenan Hudson (GL0270)
10745 Route 18
Albion, PA 16475

Dear Mr. Hudson:

I have reviewed your letter of February 26, 2016, along with the various documents you sent with the letter. Ordinarily, I make my recommendations to the Pennsylvania Board of Probation and Parole in response to a specific request they send out to sentencing judges. However, I have not received the Parole Board's request in your case, and I will soon resign from the court in order to accept another position. Therefore, I am writing this letter in response to your request. You are authorized to use this letter in connection with your application for parole.

Through our correspondence following your sentencing, you have convinced me that you are sincerely remorseful for the crime you have committed and for the life you so senselessly took. I was particular impressed by what I regard as your sincere desire to express this remorse directly to the family of the victim in your case. I do not know whether you were successful in your efforts to accomplish this, but I am convinced that your feelings were pure and expressed a real desire to make some amends for your crime.

Furthermore, in reviewing the certificates and other documents you sent me, I was very impressed with your efforts at rehabilitation and, particularly, your efforts to prepare yourself for a law abiding, productive and successful life when you are released from prison. Of course, I do not know what your full Department of Corrections records might reveal about your conduct in custody. However, assuming that there have been no serious problems in that regard over the years, I support your application for parole once you have completed your minimum sentence.

I hope this letter will be of some assistance to you.

Sincerely,

Benjamin Lerner,
Senior Judge

BL/mm

THE UNSPOKEN TRUTH

Within about 90 days, I was finally ready to go. Everything was lined up.

I couldn't sleep at night. I was giving everything away. I already had confirmation that a pastor was going to meet me. I was catching a bus. I had a ticket to get back to Philadelphia. I was going to be met by the pastor at the Greyhound station.

The secret to success is that while in prison you have to develop your own blueprint for what you want to do and how you would achieve your goals, and then do not waiver! You can't change your blueprint just because you found something that would be fun to do instead. And so like everything else I learned in my time in prison, I knew that I had to stick to my plan, review my beliefs, and I found there are attitudes and habits you can cultivate to make your transition to your future more successful. I am sharing them with you here.

BELIEVE IN YOURSELF

I know that I am going to be very successful. I DECLARE IT! That was my mantra. I came home in October 2016. At the end of this year, it's six years. The things I've accomplished in six years, most people don't accomplish in 40 years of living. They've never bought property, established credit, been in good standing with banks that, by the way, don't want you to be in good standing—they want you to be in a state of check to check. But I knew I could do it. I had faith in myself. When you have faith in yourself, a funny thing happens. Other people have faith in you, too. That's when you get opportunities.

83

SUPPORT SYSTEM

When you think of your support system, it's always going to be someone other than yourself. A crutch to lean on. When you're about to come out of prison, you've been away for so long, you have to have crutches. We're interdependent. You're going to need some kind of help. I reached out and some people ignored me. They really didn't have anything to offer. A lot of things had changed.

No one is going to open the doors for you. You don't have any previous work history. You can't provide tax returns. Housing will discriminate as quickly as jobs will, so you need people who will hold you up when you're down, support you while you're learning the ropes.

But a support system is more than just a house and employment and a thousand dollars in your pocket. You have to have someone show you how life works—how to open a bank account, how to drive, how to go grocery shopping, how to get a money order, how to budget your money, how to find health care.

MINDSET

Be determined, despite any negative energies that come against you. You have to have a mindset that says, "It's going to get done despite any opposition."

If you come up in poverty, that's how you're going to think. When you're influenced by the wrong people, you're going to be wrong, but you can change that by changing your mindset.

I know I'm going to have a trillion dollars. That's a determined

THE UNSPOKEN TRUTH

mindset. I know how to play music, monetize my music. I can transcribe music, I can read it. I was away for 15 years and styles changed, but I learned the new styles. I created a business out of it. My mindset was I don't want to live check to check. I'm a top dog, I'm elite, I'm a king.

I had a picture that, no matter what, I was going to be successful. In jail everything is predictable. Out here, nothing is. You got to be flexible.

I use social media, but I don't live there. Facebook illusions. Those are mindset illusions. However, those social media platforms can be beneficial if used the correct way.

CIRCLE EVALUATION

You are a part of your environment. Show me your friends, I'll show you your future. Bad company corrupts good morals. When you look at that, whoever you follow either in real life or social media, whoever influences you, you're going to adapt to whatever they're into. If you're around millionaires, you're going to be a millionaire. Knowing who is going to push you to the next level, accountability partners. If you don't have that, you're destined to fail. Discern whether people are for or against you, Or are you there for that moment.

Reading is a form of influence, who you read is part of your circle—MLK, Nelson Mandela, Malcom X, to name a few. I read a lot of them when I was inside. They had so much influence on me, on how they flexed their influence, especially when they came out of prison. It was like my motivation to go to that next level.

The Sunday before I left, they asked me to say some words at the

KEENAN HUDSON

church. We had a lot of different types of people. I controlled a lot of the music, so they knew me. I spoke about a lot of things for about three minutes. I made it out. If I did it, you could do it, too. I knew my time was here and I was going to make the most of it. The door was open. I got a standing ovation.

The next Thursday I was released. That morning I put on the new set of clothes I had sent up. But these clothes were so big. I had lost a lot of weight in prison, more than a hundred pounds. I had changed a lot.

So, there I was, ready to be released into the world that to my mind had stopped 15 years before. I had lots of ideas, lots of time to figure out who I would be when I got my chance, and lots of plans. I also had lots of time to set my resolve. I remember being determined more than anything. But I'm not going to kid you. For most people, re-entering society is scary. It's one thing to make plans, another thing to deal with the uncertainties of life on the outside. It takes more courage to face that uncertainty than it does to commit any crime. Lots of people can't deal with it, and they're back in.

But I believed in myself. I had the right mindset and I surrounded myself with winners and a good support system. So, with my plans in hand and my faith in God, I stepped out. I was a free man.

AFTERWARDS

....To Here

Telling you about what happened to me when I left prison is a whole other story. Another book which is coming out soon. I will tell you, though, that there is a big difference between plans on paper which stay the same, and how those plans play out in the real world, which is always changing.

My mentor, Pastor Alex, picked me up at the bus station. He had arranged for housing for me as well as a job. That being provided, the deal was I had to pay all the money outlay back. I kept saying to myself that just because you have a felony is no excuse to not succeed, but I have to admit, I did have a good set up when I got back out. My mentor let me stay in a basement apartment and work in one of his businesses, a daycare center, but I did have to return the payment.

I did return all the payments, and when things changed, circumstances changed, I had to leave and search for different opportunities. Where I worked in that first situation, daycare, where I was custodian and security, there were a lot of women and they were looking at me like I was fresh meat. Who is this guy? I had such a fresh glow. I had to adjust to that.

I had by this time the skills to move on, and for that I will always be grateful. I went from making nothing to minimum wage to six figures.

KEENAN HUDSON

My attitude was always, "I'm going to show you why I'm an asset and not a liability." That's why I advance in any career I enter. Determination. Having a heart.

By the grace of God, today I have several successful businesses, and I am my own boss. My success depends on me alone. My purpose in life is to help people who were in my situation and guide them to their own success, whether it be in music, finance, real estate, business or just living.

Sometimes people ask me if I'm bitter because I was incarcerated for a long period of time for a crime I was involved in. They say the system was stacked against me and how can I not be bitter. But I say no. Everything that happened to me has made me stronger. Everything that happened to me has made me smarter. It was a difficult education, but I graduated with honors. I think that it doesn't matter how you get to the starting gate. It just matters that you get there. I did it and you can, too. I am a firm believer that all things work together for the good.

And I am here. I am out of the starting gate and running the race. I am destined for great things. I am a king. And with God's continued favor, I will achieve greatness.

All praise be to God.

Photo from now

> This photo shows you how my faith, determination, and belief in myself created opportunities for me after I got released. I was invited to a function in Philadelphia. Vice President Biden, Governor Wolf (in the photo), and all the politicians of Philly were there.

APPENDIX

Key statements in full to Philadelphia homicide detectives that led to Probable Cause affidavit for the arrest of Keenan Hudson.

Justin Frazier

INVESTIGATION INTERVIEW RECORD	PHILADELPHIA POLICE DEPARTMENT HOMICIDE DIVISION			CASE # M04-081 INTERVIEWER: Det.John Cahill #919	
NAME Justin Christopher FRAZIER	AGE 16	RACE B	SEX M	DOB 4-27-87	
ADDRESS 7431 N. 20th St.,Phila.,PA 19138	APARTMENT #			PHONE #	
NAME OF EMPLOYMENT/SCHOOL M.L.King H/S				SSN#	
ADDRESS OF EMPLOYMENT/SCHOOL Stenton and Haines	DEPARTMENT 11th Grade			PHONE #	
DATES OF PLANNED VACATIONS					
DATES OF PLANNED BUSINESS TRIPS					
NAME OF CLOSE RELATIVE Mother: Caroline FRAZIER 39/b/f					
ADDRESS same				PHONE# same	
PLACE OF INTERVIEW Homicide Rm 104 Police Hqts	DATE 4-21-04			TIME 1255pm	
BROUGHT IN BY P/O Bowdren #1132 14th Dist	DATE 4-21-04			TIME 1150am	
WE ARE QUESTIONING YOU CONCERNING The murder by shooting of the pizza delivery man at 7407 Andrews Ave on 3-28-04					
WARNINGS GIVEN BY Det. John Cahill #919	DATE 4-21-04			TIME 1255pm	

ANSWERS

(1) yes   (2) yes   (3) no   (4) yes   (5) yes   (6) no   (7) yes

Q1. Justin I am Det Cahill of the Homicide Division and I have advised you of the possible charges against you and I have warned you of your Constitutional Rights and I have tried to contact your father, Jeffrey FUNCHESS at the phone number you gave me which is ⸗ and there was no answer and you have indicated to me that you wish to make a statement concerning this incident without first speaking with your father is that correct?
A1. Yes.   J.F

Q2. What is your mother's name?
A2. Caroline FRAZIER 39/b/f.   J.F   Ashley

Q3. Does she live with you?
A3. Yes she lives with me but she is presently away at drug rehab.   J.F

Q4. Do you know where the rehab is or do you have a phone number of where she can be reached at?
A4. It is somewhere in Kensington. I don't know her phone number.   J.F

Q5. Does your father work?
A5. Yes he works at McFadden's Restaurant at the new stadium.   J.F

Q6. Justin I have tried to contact your father at work at   and there is no answer. Do you still wish to continue with your statement at this time?
A6. Yes.   J.F

RECORD [ ] YES [ ] NO	CHECKED BY:
REVIEWED BY:	

75-483

STATEMENT OF: Justin Frazier

DATE AND TIME: 4-21-04 1255 Pm

PLACE: Homicide Unit Rm 104 PAB

CONCERNING: The Shooting Death of Abraham Cisse 26/B/m on 3-28-04 at 7407 Andrews An

IN PRESENCE OF:

INTERROGATED BY: Det Cahill #919

RECORDED BY:

I am Det Cahill of the Homicide Division

We are questioning you concerning The Murder By Shooting of a Pizza Delivery Man on 3-28-04 at 7407 Andrews Ave.

We have a duty to explain to you and to warn you that you have the following legal rights:

A. You have a right to remain silent and do not have to say anything at all.

B. Anything you say can and will be used against you in Court.

C. You have a right to talk to a lawyer of your own choice before we ask you any questions, and also to have a lawyer here with you while we ask questions.

D. If you cannot afford to hire a lawyer, and you want one, we will see that you have a lawyer provided to you, free of charge, before we ask you any questions.

E. If you are willing to give us a statement, you have a right to stop any time you wish.

5-331 D (Rev. 7/70)

Page 1

1. Q. Do you understand that you have a right to keep quiet, and do not have to say anything at all?

   A. YES J.F

2. Q. Do you understand that anything you say can and will be used against you?

   A. YES J.F

3. Q. Do you want to remain silent?

   A. NO J.F

4. Q. Do you understand that you have a right to talk with a lawyer before we ask you any questions?

   A. YES J.F

5. Q. Do you understand that if you cannot afford to hire a lawyer, and you want one, we will not ask you any questions until a lawyer is appointed for you free of charge.

   A. YES J.F

6. Q. Do you want to talk with a lawyer at this time, or to have a lawyer with you while we ask you questions?

   A. NO J.F

7. Q. Are you willing to answer questions of your own free will, without force or fear, and without any threats or promises having been made to you?

   A. YES JF

Statement of: Date: 4-21-04 12:55 pm

INVESTIGATION INTERVIEW RECORD	CITY OF PHILADELPHIA
CONTINUATION SHEET	POLICE DEPARTMENT

Q7. Tell me in your own words what you know about the robbery and shooting of the pizza deliveryman on Sunday 3-28-04 at 7407 Andrews Ave?

A7. It all started earlier that day. Me, Marty, Biggs, Stephan and some other young boys were playing B-ball at Lynwood Gardens in Cheltenham and Biggs started say things like "we need a car, we need some money, we need to rob somebody" and we paid him no mind and we just chilled in the neighborhood for the rest of the day. Later I walked to the Chinese store on Ogontz to get a loose cigarette and then I walked to Marty's house and when I got to Marty's house, Biggs, Marty and Stephan were sitting on the steps and they were still talking about robbing somebody. Biggs said that they were going to order a pizza and he then said that they were going to rob the pizza man. We then went into the house and Biggs called in the pizza order and then we went outside and we went down to the corner. We were down there for about fifteen minutes and when the man didn't come Biggs and Marty went back and called the pizza place again. J.F

Q8. Did you go back with Marty and Biggs to make the call?
A8. No me and Stephan stayed on the corner. J.F

Q9. What happened next?
A9. We waited for the man to come but it was taking a long time and I didn't think the man was going to come and I said that we should just forget about it and Biggs was saying we need the money. J.F

Q10. About how long did you wait on the corner for the pizza man to arrive?
A10. It was a long time. I know it was getting late because I had to be in my house at nine olock and I was just ready to walk home when the pizza man showed up. J.F

Q11. What happened when the pizza man showed up?
A11. My heart dropped when he drove up and I knew it was him. Biggs then told me that I know what me job was and that was to take the man's car. The man got out of his car and he walked towards the house and then Biggs bear hugged him and I heard either Biggs or Marty yell "give it up, give it up" and then I think they were wrestling with the guy and then I started walking up Andrews and before I got to the driveway I heard "POW" and I just ran up the alley and went to my house. S.F

Q12. Where were you at during the robbery?
A12. I was on the corner (indicating on the map the NWC of 74th and Andrews). J.F

Q13. Where were Marty and Biggs at during the robbery?
A13. They were right in front of the house where the man got shot at. J.F

Q14. Where was Stephan at during the robbery?
A14. He was a couple of house up from where Marty and Biggs was. S.F

Q15. Why were you on the corner during the robbery?
A15. I was there to look out for the cops and to take the guys car. J.F

Q16. Do you at this time need to use the bathroom or want something to eat or drink?
A16. No I'm good. J.F

Q17. What type or food did Biggs order?
A17. He ordered two pizza's and two cheese steaks and I don't know what else. J.F

Q18. What happened when you got back to your house?
A18. Me Marty and Stephan got back there first and then Biggs knocked on my door and he showed us the money that he took off of the guy and then he heard the sirens and he said "yo man I'm scared I don't know what to do" and I told him to go home. Before he left he gave the money to Marty. J.F

Q19. How much money did Biggs give Marty?
A19. It was a lot of quarters and a couple of dollars in paper money. J.F

RECORD [ ] YES [ ] NO	CHECKED BY: *Justin Fragan*
REVIEWED BY:	

75-483

INVESTIGATION INTERVIEW RECORD	CITY OF PHILADELPHIA
CONTINUATION SHEET	POLICE DEPARTMENT

Q20. About how much in coins was there?
A20. It looked like about four dollars. J F

Q21. What did Marty do with the money?
A21. About fifteen minutes later he went to the store and bought cigarettes and then we went back to my house and sat on the steps. J F

Q22. Was there anything else taken from the pizza man?
A22. Only the food. J F

Q23. Who took the food?
A23. I don't know who took it but it was at my steps when I got there. J F

Q24. Did you eat any of the food.
A24. No I didn't feel good so I didn't eat any of it. J F

Q25. What is Biggs full name?
A25. Keenan, I don't know his last name. J F

Q26. What is Stephan's full name?
A26. I don't know his last name. J F

Q27. Describe Stephan to me?
A27. He is around 16 yrs old., and he lives somewhere on Walnut Lane around 75th. He is about 5'6" 145lbs and my complexion (MBRN). J J

Q28. How long have you know Biggs?
A28. About four weeks. J F

Q29. How long have you known Stephan?
A29. Since like two summers ago. J F

Q30. Did you know that Marty had a gun on him during the robbery of the pizza man?
A30. Yes. J F

Q31. What kind of gun did he have?
A31. I don't know my gun types. J F

Q32. Did you ever see his gun?
A32. Yes I saw it about a week before. J F

Q33. What did the gun look like?
A33. It was dark colored with brown in it. J F

Q34. Do you know Kareem Daughtry?
A34. Yes he is Marty's brother. J F

Q35. Was Kareem Daughtry involved in this incident at all?
A36. No. J F

Q37. Do you know Robert Shair White?
A37. Yes. J F

Q38. Was Robert involved in this incident at all?
A38. No. J F

RECORD [ ] YES [ ] NO	CHECKED BY: *Justin Zuang un*
REVIEWED BY:	

75-483

PAGE #4 OF

INVESTIGATION INTERVIEW RECORD
CONTINUATION SHEET

CITY OF PHILADELPHIA
POLICE DEPARTMENT

Q39. Did you see Kareem Daughtry the night of the robbery/murder?
A39. No. J.F

Q40. Did you see Robert White the night of the robbery/murder?
A40. I saw him earlier that night but he left before it went down. J.F

Q41. Why didn't you take the pizza man's car?
A41. I was scared and then when I heard the shot I just ran. J.F

Q42. Did you ever go into or near the pizza man's car?
A42. No. J.F

Q43 Did you see anybody go into the man's car?
A43. No. J.F
   who J.F
Q44. Did shot the pizza man?
A44. Marty did. J.F

Q45. Did Marty ever tell you why he shot the pizza man?
A45. No. J.F

Q46. Justin what grade are you in?
A46. I'm in 11th grade at M L King High School. J.F

Q47. Do you read write and understand English?
A47. Yes. J.F

Q48. Are you presently under the influence of drugs or alcohol?
A48. No. J.F

Q49. Are you willing to read this statement which consist of (4) pages and sign it if it is true and correct?
A49. Yes. J.F

Q50. Is there anything else that you want to tell me about this incident?
A50. I wish this never happened. I feel sorry for the man who got killed. I didn't know that Marty was going to shoot him and I apologize my friend's actions. J.F

Q51. Justin this is Det. Mellon #9029 and he is going to show you a photo array consisting of (8) photographs and you have identified photo #7 is that correct?
A51. Yes. J.F

Q52. Who is photograph #7 a picture of?
A52. That is BIGGS. J.F

Q53. Is that the same Biggs that you know who participated in the robbery and murder of the pizza delivery man on 3-28-04 at 7407 Andrews Ave?
A53. Yes. J.F

Justin Fragun 4-21-04
2:17 pM

RECORD [ ] YES [ ] NO	CHECKED BY:
REVIEWED BY:	

75-483

Kareem Daughtry

INVESTIGATION INTERVIEW RECORD	PHILADELPHIA POLICE DEPARTMENT HOMICIDE UNIT		CASE # M(INTERVIEV Det.John (
NAME Kareem DAUGHTRY	AGE 17	RACE B	SEX M	DOB 11-24-8(

NAME Kareem DAUGHTRY	AGE 17	RACE B	SEX M	DOB 11-24-8(
ADDRESS 1967 74TH Ave.,Phila.,PA	APARTMENT #			PHONE #
NAME OF EMPLOYMENT/SCHOOL Valley Day				SSN#
ADDRESS OF EMPLOYMENT/SCHOOL Morrisville PA	DEPARTMENT			PHONE #
DATES OF PLANNED VACATIONS				
DATES OF PLANNED BUSINESS TRIPS				
NAME OF CLOSE RELATIVE Patricia MASON 62/b/f				
ADDRESS 1102 E. Sharpnack St.,Phila.,PA 19150				PHONE#
PLACE OF INTERVIEW HOMICIDE	DATE 3-31-04			TIME 120AM
BROUGHT IN BY	DATE			TIME

WE ARE QUESTIONING YOU CONCERNING
The murder of a pizza delivery man on Sunday 3-28-04.

WARNINGS GIVEN BY	DATE	TIME

ANSWERS
(1)   (2)   (3)   (4)   (5)   (6)

Q1. I am Det.Cahill of the Homicide Unit and I would like to ask you some questions about what if anything that yo of a pizza delivery man on Sunday 3-28-04 at 7407 Andrews Ave?
A1. OK.

Q2. Tell me in your own words what you know about this incident?
A2. I was in my house asleep and I heard some people talking downstairs and I got up and I went downstairs and wl Martique and Biggs and there were other people there but I didn't see who they were. I could hear Martique taking asking people what they wanted. Then Biggs said whats up Reem and I looked at him and I didn't say anything to h upstairs.

Q3. What time was this?
A3. It was around 7 or 8pm.

Q4. Where was Martique and Biggs when you saw them?
A4. They were on the first floor in the living room.

Q5. What happened next?
A5. I went back to sleep and then I remember my dad waking me up and he asked me if I knew what was going on c him to leave me the fuck alone and I went right back to sleep.

Q6. What is the next thing that you remember?
A6. I got up around 7am on Monday and I went downstairs and my dad told me that Martique did something on the him to stop playing and I started making an egg sandwich and then I went back up to my room and my Uncle Clock he told me that the pizza guy got killed on the corner and that Martique had something to do with it. Me and him we front steps and he said that he was glad that I wasn't involved in it.

RECORD [ ] YES [ ] NO	CHECKED BY:
REVIEWED BY:	

75-483

INVESTIGATION INTERVIEW RECORD		CITY OF PHILADELPHIA
CONTINUATION SHEET		**P O L I C E D E P A R T M E N T**

Q7. Did you Uncle Clock mention any other names of the people involved in killing the pizza man.
A7. No he just mentioned Martique.

Q8. What is Uncle Clocks real name?
A8. John LAWSON.

Q9. What happened next?
A9. Michelle called my house and she was talking to Grandmom and I called her back and I asked her what was going on and she told me that Miss Lillian told her that Miss Lillians children were taken out of her house on Venango St by the police. I then called Miss Lillian and I asked her what happened to the kids and she told me that the police came and took them and I asked her where Casha was and she told me he was at school. She asked me if I had anything to do with the pizza man and I told her no and then she asked me if Martique had anything to do with it and I told her I didn't know. After that I called Robert White (Shyeer) and he told me that he was on the corner when he saw Martique and Bigg's with the pizza guy and he said that Bigg's was playing with the gun at the man's head and that the gun went off and shot the man in the head and then Shyeer said that Martique and Bigg's ran and then he also ran and he ran to my house and my Uncle Clock let him into the house and he said that he got his stuff and he left and went home. I then went out and I looked for Martique and I saw this guy name Mel, he didn't have anything to do with it, and I got into his car and we drove around and we found Martique walking down the street, I don't remember the name of the street, and I asked him what happened and Martique told me that him and Bigg's robbed the pizza guy and that the guy gave him $30.00 and Martique took the food and then Bigg's shot the guy in the head and then they both ran away. I told him that he should go and hide because the police won't believe him and he then left.

Q10. When was the next time that you saw Martique?
A10. No I haven't seen or spoken to him since Monday.

Q11. What is Bigg's real name?
A11. I think it is Kev or Kevin I'm not sure. He lives somewhere on Plymouth St.

Q12. When was the last time that you saw Bigg's?
A12. The last time I saw him was the night of the incident when I woke up ans saw him in my livingroom.

Q13. When did you go to the house on Venango St?
A13. I went there Saturday night.

Q14. How did you get there.
A14. I took my bike on the El and I got off at Allegheny and I rode my bike to the house.

Q15. What did you do after you got to the Venango St house?
A15. We walked around a little bit and then I went back to the house and I laid down because I was tired and I went to sleep.

Q16. Did you have a converstion with anyone inside the house about scaming a pizza man.
A16. No.

Q17. Did you hear anyone else talking about scaming a pizza man?
A17. No.

Q18. After you fell asleep when did you wake back up?
A18. I didn't wake up until Sunday morning.

Q18. What did you do when you woke up?
A18. I cooked some oddles of noodles and I went out with Jamilla and some other girl and then when we got back to the house and I took a showere and then me and Martique got on our bikes and we drove home.

Q19. Did you ever see Martique with a gun while you were at the Venango St house?
A19. No.

RECORD	CHECKED BY:
[ ] YES [ ] NO	
REVIEWED BY:	
75-483	

| INVESTIGATION INTERVIEW RECORD | CITY OF PHILADELPHIA |
| CONTINUATION SHEET | POLICE DEPARTMENT |

Q20. Do you know of any other pizza men robberies in your neighborhood.
A20. No.

Q21. Do you know if Martique did any other robberies?
A21. No.

Q22. Does Martique have a key to the house?
A22. Yes.

Q23. Did you tell anyone at school about the pizza man being killed?
A23. Yes.

Q24. Who did you tell?
A24. I told my counselor on Tuesday.

Q25. What is your counselor's name?
A25. Ann SCHIVONNI (Phonetic)

Q26. What did you tell her?
A26. I asked her if she saw the news about the pizza man being killed and she said yes and I told her that I think my little brother (Martique) was involved in it.

Q27. Did you tell her that Martique had shot the pizza man?
A27. I might have and I might not have.

Q28. What did you wear when you went to the Venango St house on Saturday?
A28. I wore a black dickie outfit with a du-rag on.

Q29. What did you wear when you left the house on Sunday?
A29. I wore these pants (blue jeans with writing on the legs) and a blue shirt with stripes and a black jacket with a fur hood.

Q30 What was Martique wearing when he left the Venango St house?
A30. A red shirt and some kind of monkey or gorilla mask on his face. I don't remember what else he was wearing.

Q31. Where did he get the mask from?
A31. He took it from Casha's room.

Q32. Where does Robert WHITE live?
A32. Somewhere near King High School.

Q33. What was taken off of the pizza man?
A33. Two pizza's, 2 cheese steaks and buffalo wings. $30.00 in cash and a set of keys.

Q34. Who told you what was taken from the man?
A34. Martique told me what was taken.

Q35. What happened to the money?
A35. Martique told me that they spent it on weed.

Q36. What happened to the keys?
A36. Martique said that they bleeched them because it had his finger prints on them and I don't know what he did with them after that.

Q37. Did you eat any of the food that was taken?
A37. No

| RECORD [ ] YES [ ] NO | CHECKED BY: |
| REVIEWED BY: | |

75-483

PAGE #4 OF

| INVESTIGATION INTERVIEW RECORD | CITY OF PHILADELPHIA |
| CONTINUATION SHEET | P O L I C E   D E P A R T M E N T |

Q38. What happened to the gun?
A38. I don't know. Martique might have sold it.

Q39. Did you have anything to do with the planning of and carrying out the robbery and shooting of the pizza delivery man?
A39. No.

Q40. Do you know who made the phone call for the pizza?
A40. I don't know.

Q41. Is there anything else that you want to tell me?
A41. No I told you everything that I know.

Q42. After reading over this statement with your step mother, Patricia Mason, are you willing to consent to have this interview video taped?
A42. No I don't want it video taped.

Raheem Daughtey
Pat. Mason   3·31·04   3⁵⁸ p.m.

RECORD	CHECKED BY:
[ ] YES [ ] NO	
REVIEWED BY:	

75-483

Martique Daughtry

INVESTIGATION INTERVIEW RECORD	PHILADELPHIA POLICE DEPARTMENT HOMICIDE DIVISION	CASE NUMBER M04-51
		INTERVIEWER Cummings / Cahil"

NAME Martique DAUGHTRY	AGE 16	RACE B/M	DOB 2-15-88
ADDRESS 1967 74th Ave.,Phila.,PA 19138	APARTMENT NUMBER		TELEPHONE NUMBER
NAME OF EMPLOYMENT/SCHOOL			SOCIAL SECURITY NUMBER
ADDRESS OF EMPLOYMENT/SCHOOL	DEPARTMENT		TELEPHONE NUMBER
DATES OF PLANNED VACATIONS			
DATES OF PLANNED BUSINESS TRIPS			
NAME OF CLOSE RELATIVE			
ADDRESS			TELEPHONE NUMBER

PLACE OF INTERVIEW Police Hqts Rm 104 Interview room B	DATE 4-1-04	TIME 3:10p
BROUGHT IN BY	DATE 4-1-04	TIME 1:25p
WE ARE QUESTIONING YOU CONCERNING The murder by shooting of a pizza delivery man on 3-28-04 at 7407 Andrews Ave.		
WARNINGS GIVEN BY Det. Cummings	DATE 4-1-04	TIME 3:05pm

ANSWERS   (1) Yes   (2) Yes   (3) No   (4) Yes   (5) Yes   (6) No   (7) Yes

Q1. Martique I am Det Cahill and this is Det Cummings and I have advised you of the charges a
you have been warned of your constitutional rights and you have spoken with your father,
Robert Daughtry, and after speaking with your father do you at this time wish to make a
statement concerning this matter?
A1. Yes. MD

Q. How far did you go in school?

A. I am in thr 9th now at M.L.K. MD

Q. Can you read, write and understand the English language?

A. Yes. MD

Q. After speaking with your Father, do you still wish to talk with us?

A. Yes. MD

COORD ☐ Yes ☐ No	CHECKED BY
VIEWED BY	

-483 (Rev. 7/82)

INVESTIGATION INTERVIEW RECORD	CITY OF PHILADELPHIA	
CONTINUATION SHEET	POLICE DEPARTMENT	

NAME Martique DAUGHTRY

PAGE 2   CASE NO. M04-81

Q. Were you present on Sunday, 3-29-04 at 7407 Andrews Ave when a pizza delivery man was she and killed?

A. Yes. MD

Q. Who shot the pizza delivery man?

A. 1 did. MD

Q. What type of gun did you use to shoot the pizza delivery man?

A. A 380. MD

Q. Who owns the gun that you shot the delivery man with?

A. 1 took it from Kareem LAWSON where he was staying. MD

Q. How do you know Kareem?

A. From the neighborhood. MD

Q. Did Kareem know that you took his gun?

A. Yeah. MD

Q. Were you alone when you shot the delivery man?

A. No. 1 was with BIGS. MD

Q. Do you know BIGs' real name?

A. Not his last name but his first name is CALVIN. MD

33A

INVESTIGATION INTERVIEW RECORD
CONTINUATION SHEET

CITY OF PHILADELPHIA
POLICE DEPARTMENT

NAME: Martique DAUGHTRY

PAGE: 3

CASE NO.: M04-81

Q. Where is that gun at now?

A. 1 gave it back to Kareem. MD

Q. Was the gun in a holster?

A. When I took it it was in a holster but then I lost it and I gave it back it didn't have a holster. MD

Q. Go on in your own words and tell us what happened?

A. 1 was in Kensington all weekend and on Sunday I went back up my way on Sunday. We was all on the top of 74th St just chilling. Then we went to my crib and was just chilling for the the rest of the day. All day BIGS was talking about robbing people saying that he needed money. He was like Marty you might as well just do cause you got to eat anyway. MD

Q. Did you tell BIGS that you had a gun?

A. He all ready knew. MD

So then he called the pizza man. He called the pizza place and told me to place the order so BIGS told them that he wanted 2 pizzas, 2 cheese steaks and a 30 piece wings. Then the guy didn't show so BIGS called again. He called like 4 times. The pizza place wanted a call back number, so 1 gave BIGS a number down in knesington and BIGS gave it to them. MD

Q. What was the phone number in Kensington?

A. MD

Q. Did you call that number to let the people in Kensington about the pizza order?

A. Yeah 1 just said that if someione calls about food just say yeah. MD

Martique Daughtry Martique Daughtry Edw Daughty

| INVESTIGATION INTERVIEW RECORD | CITY OF PHILADELPHIA |
| CONTINUATION SHEET | POLICE DEPARTMENT |

NAME Martique DAUGHTRY

PAGE 4 CASE NO. M04-81

Q. Who did you speak with at   ?

A. Jamilla, a fake cousin. My Mom anf her Mom are best friends. MD

Q. What happened after you placed the order?

A. We went down the street and waited for the pizza man? MD

Q. Where was the food to be delivered?

A. BIGS told them a house on Andrews. MD

Q. Who's house was the food to be delivered to?

A. l don't know, I didn't know the people there we needed a address. MD

Q. What ahppened after the pizza man arrived?

A. The pizza man got out the car and walked over to the house then BIGS said to the pizzaman
just knock on the door. Then BIGS followed him and when the pizzaman passed BIGS, BIGS
grabbed him from behind. Then BIGS said to me come on man do your job and l pulled out
the gun and put it to the guys head. The guy wasn't moving than BIGS must have done
something or something and the gun went off. I just dropped the gun and it fell on the food
and l picked up the food and the gun and ran. I ran up Sterling towards Justin's house
and went inside Justin's house. MD

Q. How many times did you shoot the pizza man?

A. Once. MD

Q. Are you right handed or left handed?

83A

Martique Daughtry   Martique Daughtry   Pl Dagly

| INVESTIGATION INTERVIEW RECORD | CITY OF PHILADELPHIA |
| CONTINUATION SHEET | POLICE DEPARTMENT |

| NAME | | PAGE | CASE NO. |
| Martique DAUGHTRY | | 5 | MD4-81 |

A. Lefthanded. MD

Q. What hand did you have the gun in when you fired?

A. My left. MD

Q. Did the pizza man say anything to you?

A. No. MD

Q. Did BIGS get any of the food?

A. No 1 took everything and ran. MD

Q. Did the pizza man gave a weapon?

A. No. MD

Q. Who told the pizza man to give it up?

A. 1 just told the pizzaman to freeze while 1 had the gun up. MD

Q. Where does Kareem LAWSON live?

A. He was living on Ronova st. MD

Q. When did you take the gun?

A. Like two weeks ago. MD

Q. Did you have a conversation about robbing a pizzaman while you were in Kensington?

A. 1 was there when SHA, DORAL, JAMILLA was talking about trying to rob a pizzaman, One MD

3A

INVESTIGATION INTERVIEW RECORD
CONTINUATION SHEET

CITY OF PHILADELPHIA
POLICE DEPARTMENT

NAME: Martique DAUGHTRY

PAGE: 6

CASE NO.: M04-81

of the girls called a pizza place and asked me for a address cause that didn't want for the food to come to their house 1 didn't say nothing so the girl who called hung up. MD

Q. Did you have the gun on you that day?

A. Yes. MD

Q. When the pizza man showed up on Andrews, dod you cock the hammer back?

A. 1 pulled the whole top back and it cocked. MD

Q. When you pulled the top back, did a bullet come out?

A. Yes. MD

Q. What were you wearing that night?

A. Some blue jeans and a black shirt a blue coat with a fir collar. MD

Q. Were you wearing a mask that night?

A. No, but I had a Gorilla mask eariler that day. MD

Q. Describe BIGS?

A. He is about 16 or 17 big like over 6' like 285 lbs MD

Q. Marty, we would like you to read this 6 page statement and if it is true and correct sign each page. Ok?

A. Ok. MD

Martique Daughtry

3A

Martiques Daughtry   *Robt Daughtry*

Robert Shair White

INVESTIGATION INTERVIEW RECORD				PHILADELPHIA POLICE DEPARTMENT HOMICIDE DIVISION		CASE # M04-081 INTERVIEWER: Det.John Cahill #919
NAME Robert Shair WHITE				AGE 15	RACE B	SEX M	DOB 7-9-88
ADDRESS 6700 Hollis St.,Phila.,PA				APARTMENT #		PHONE #
NAME OF EMPLOYMENT/SCHOOL Martin Luther King H/S						SSN#
ADDRESS OF EMPLOYMENT/SCHOOL Stenton and Haines				DEPARTMENT 10th		PHONE #
DATES OF PLANNED VACATIONS						
DATES OF PLANNED BUSINESS TRIPS						
NAME OF CLOSE RELATIVE Mother: Darlene White 39/b/f						
ADDRESS same						PHONE# same
PLACE OF INTERVIEW HOMICIDE				DATE 4-20-04		TIME 1115am
BROUGHT IN BY Pol.				DATE 4-20-04		TIME 1110am
WE ARE QUESTIONING YOU CONCERNING The murder by shooting of Abraham CISSE 26/b/m at 7407 Andrews Ave on 3-28-04.						
WARNINGS GIVEN BY				DATE		TIME

ANSWERS

(1)	(2)	(3)	(4)	(5)	(6)	(7)

Q1. Robert I am Det Cahill of the Homicide Division and I would like to ask you some questions about what you know about the shooting and murder of the pizza delivery man on 3-28-04 at 7407 Andrews Ave?
A1. OK.

Q2. Tell me in your own words what you know about this incident?
A2. I was walking home from my girls house and it was around 9pm and I was walking up 74th Ave towards Andrews and just before I got to Andrews Ave I heard a shot and when I got to the corner of 74th and Andrews Ave I saw a b/m crossing Andrews Ave and the male looked back at me and then I just ran up to Marty's house.

Q3. Do you remember seeing a car in the middle of Andrews Ave?
A3. Yes I saw a car with flashing lights on.

Q4. Did you see anyone in the car?
A4. No.

Q5. Where was the male that you saw crossing Andrews Ave in relation to the car with the flashers on?
A5. He was directly across from where the car was parked.

Q6. Before you ran up to Marty's house did you see anyone else on the street around 74th and Andrews Ave?
A6. The only other people that I saw were two men on bikes, one was white and the other was dark skin and they were on the other side of 74th and they were riding there bikes towards 20th St. Skin R.W.

Q7. Do you know either of the men on the bikes?
A7. No.

RECORD [ ] YES [ ] NO	CHECKED BY: Robert White
REVIEWED BY:	

75-483

INVESTIGATION INTERVIEW RECORD	CITY OF PHILADELPHIA
CONTINUATION SHEET	P O L I C E D E P A R T M E N T

Q8. Can you describe the male who you saw crossing the street by the car with the flashers on?
A8. He was a young guy about 15 yrs old and he is about 6'1" and he is heavy set over 200lbs and he has dark skin and he was wearing dark clothes.

Q9. Do you know this males name?
A9. They call him BIGGS.

Q10. Have you ever seen Biggs before that night?
A10. Yes.

Q11. When was the last time that you saw Biggs before that night?
A11. It was that same night around 730pm or 8pm and I was at Marty's house and there were about nine guys there and they were hanging on the porch and the front step and one of the guys might have been Biggs.

Q12. What were you doing at Marty's house?
A12. I was talking to my girl on the house phone and I told her to meet me at Marty's house and then I met her outside and we played around on the corner for a little bit and then I saw Marty and some of the other guys walking down towards Andrews and Marty was in the front and then my girl said that she wanted to go home, so I walked her to her house on Bouvier St.

Q13. How long were you at Marty's house before your girl arrived?
A13. I got there about 6pm and I fell asleep for a little while on the couch and they I woke up when my girl called my cell phone around 7pm.

Q14. Do you know BIGGS real name?
A14. Keenan.

Q15. Have you ever seen Biggs before Sunday 3-28-04?
A15. I saw him three days before at 20th and 73rd.

Q16. How long have you known Marty?
A16. Since an infant.

Q17. How long have you known Kareem Daughtry?
A17. Since last summer.

Q18. Did you see Kareem Daughtry at anytime on 3-28-04?
A18. I saw him earlier that day about 12pm or 1pm at 20th and 73rd and I didn't see him again that day.

Q19. While you were at Marty's house before you met your girlfriend, did you hear anyone talking about ordering pizza and wings?
A19. No.

Q20. After you heard the gunshot and you ran to Marty's house, who was there when you arrived?
A20. His grandmom was in her bedroom and his uncle Clock was in the kitchen. I asked clock where Marty's was and he said that he didn't know and then I asked him if he heard the gunshot at the end of the street and he said what gunshot. I then went upstairs and I asked grandmom where Marty and Kareem were at and she said that she didn't know where Marty was and that Kareem was in his bedroom asleep. I asked her if she heard the gunshot and she said no.

Q21. What did you do next?
A21. I then walked back to the corner of 74th and Andrews and as I got to the corner I saw a cop car coming up Andrews from Penfield and then I looked across the street and I saw what looked like somebody's leg sticking out from behind a bush and then the cops ran there. I then started looking for Marty and I then walked to Justin's house on 20th St and when I got there it was Justin and this other boy, I don't know his name, and I asked them if they knew where Marty's was and they didn't answer me they were just giggling and then I asked them if they knew what happened and they just kept laughing about it. I stayed there for a couple of minutes and then I went home.

RECORD [ ] YES [ ] NO	CHECKED BY: *Robert White*
REVIEWED BY:	

75-483

INVESTIGATION INTERVIEW RECORD	CITY OF PHILADELPHIA
CONTINUATION SHEET	POLICE DEPARTMENT

Q22. Did you see anyone else in Justin's house?
A22. I saw his younger sister, Ashley 12 yrs., and she let me into the house and I went down to the basement and Justin and this boy were sitting on the bed and I could see a shadow of somebody behind a door but I didn't know who it was.

Q23. If that was Marty behind the door why do you think he was hiding from you?
A23. Because he knows that I would have flipped out if I knew that he was involved with it.

Q24. When was the first time that you saw Marty after the pizzaman was shot?
A24. I saw him the next day, Monday, about 11am or 12pm and I saw him on my street and I asked him what happened last night and he said that he heard that the boy Biggs had shot the pizzaman and that he wasn't there and then he told me that he was there and that he took the pizza and ran and then about two days later he finally told me the real story and he told me that Biggs grabbed the pizzaman and that Marty was pointing the gun at the man's head and he was shaking the gun and it went off and he said that he ran up Sterling St. I asked him who all was there and Marty said that it was him, Biggs, and two other people.

Q25. Did he ever tell you who the other two people were?
A25. No.

Q26. Did you ever see Marty with a gun?
A26. Yes about a week or so before the pizzaman got shot he showed me a 380 and he said that he got it from Kareem Lawson.

Q27. What color was the gun?
A27. I think was all black with a brown handle.

Q28. Did Marty tell you what he did with the gun after the pizzaman was shot?
A28. No.

Q29. Robert I'm getting the feeling that you're not being perfectly honest with me during this statement. Is there anything else that you want to tell me at this time about what you know about the shooting of the pizza deliveryman?
A29. Yes.

Q30. What is it that you want to tell me?
A30. I'll tell you what I really know. I got to the house about 6pm and I fell asleep on the sofa and I woke up about 7pm and I called my girl on the phone and while I was talking on the phone to my girl Marty came in and he said that they going to rob a pizza man and he asked me if I wanted to do it with them and I said I don't care and he asked me to look for a menu. I started looking in the drawers for a menu and then Marty found one in the kitchen and then I got off of the phone and I went outside to meet my girl and when I got outside I saw all these guys on the steps and the porch and I walked down the corner to meet my girl and we stayed there for about 10-15 minutes.

Q31. What happened next?
A31. While I was on the corner I saw Marty, Biggs, Justin and a guy I think his name is Steff and some other guys walking down from Marty's house to Andrews. Marty told me that they were going to have the food delivered to the driveway behind the house on Andrews ave and we were all hanging out in that driveway and then Steff asked me if I was going to do it with them and I didn't answer him. I got second thoughts about doing it so me and my girl walked away and we went to Bruno's Pizza at 18th and Cheltenham and then we went to my girl's house.

Q32. What is your girls name and address?
A32. I call her Pebbles. Her name is ~~Marllina~~ BYRD 15/b/f she lives on the 7300 Block Bouvier St., .
Marlina B.W.

Q33. What happened next?
A33. I stayed at Pebbles until just around 9pm and when I left I walked up 74th and when I got to Andrews I heard the shot and I saw Biggs walking across Andrews from the car with the flashers on and I saw, it was either Justin or Steff, going up the alley between 74th and Sterling, and I saw Marty running up Andrews towards Sterling and then he ran up Sterling.

RECORD	CHECKED BY: *Robert W.B*
[ ] YES [ ] NO	
REVIEWED BY:	

75-483

INVESTIGATION INTERVIEW RECORD	CITY OF PHILADELPHIA
CONTINUATION SHEET	POLICE DEPARTMENT

Q34. What did you do then?
A34. I then ran up to Marty's house and everything I told you earlier about what happened when I got to Marty's house is true. I then returned to the corner and I saw the cops and I saw the body on the ground and then I went to Justin's house to look for Marty and when I got there I saw Justin, Steff and Marty and they were in the basement and they were talking about what happened and Marty said that Biggs had grabbed the guy and that Marty was shaking the gun and he shot the guy by accident and Justin was saying that he went through the guys car and Steff said that he took the food. The food was hidden under the bed and then Justin brought it out and we started eating it. I had a slice of pizza and then I left and went home.

Q35. When did you see Marty again?
A35. I saw him on the street on Monday. I then saw him on Tuesday afternoon and he asked me if he could keep the gun at my house and I told yes and he put it in a football play chest in my basement. Marty then left my house and a couple of hours later Marty called me I told him that I had to get the gun out of my house and I told him that I was going to put the gun in a city blue bag and I took it to the driveway behind Renova St between 20th and Andrews and I put it on a step and he told me later that he got the gun.

Q36. Do you know where the gun is now?
A36. Marty didn't tell me but the rumor is that he threw it down a sewer somewhere.

Q37. Did you have any other involvement in this murder other than you were present when it was planned, you witnessed Marty, Biggs and another person running away after the shooting, you shared in the pizza afterwards and you stored the gun for Marty and then returned it to him?
A37. That's all I did.

Q38. Was Kareem DAUGHTRY involved in this murder in anyway?
A38. No.

Q39. Is there anything else that you wish to tell me about this incident?
A39. No.

Q40. Robert what grade are you presently in at school?
A40. I'm in 10th grade.

Q41. Are you presently under the influence of drugs or alcohol?
A41. No.

Q42. Do you read write and understand English?
A42. Yes.

Q43. Are you willing to read this statement, which consist of four pages and sign it if it is true and correct?
A43. Yes.

Q44. Robert, you were just shown a photo array which consist of (8) photographs by Det.Lynch #796 and you identified photo #7 as being the photograph of the person that you know as "BIGGS" and this being the same person that you know was involved in the robbery and shooting of the pizzaman at 7407 Andrews Ave on 3-28-04 is that correct?
A44. Yes.

Robert White

4-20-04

4:22 pm

RECORD	CHECKED BY:
[ ] YES [ ] NO	
REVIEWED BY:	

75-483

SHAHEED HAITH

INVESTIGATION INTERVIEW RECORD		PHILADELPHIA POLICE DEPARTMENT HOMICIDE DIVISION			CASE # M04-81 INTERVIEWER: Dets. Cahill/Hagan	
NAME Shaheed HAITH	AGE 13	RACE b		SEX m	DOB 9-18-90	
ADDRESS 7405 Andrews Ave Phila 19138	APARTMENT #				PHONE #	
NAME OF EMPLOYMENT/SCHOOL Roosevelt Middle School					SSN#	
ADDRESS OF EMPLOYMENT/SCHOOL	DEPARTMENT				PHONE #	
DATES OF PLANNED VACATIONS						
DATES OF PLANNED BUSINESS TRIPS						
NAME OF CLOSE RELATIVE Grand Mother: Dorothea Miller 51/b/f						
ADDRESS same					PHONE# same	
PLACE OF INTERVIEW Homicide Rm 104 Police Hqts	DATE 5-10-04				TIME 735pm	
BROUGHT IN BY Dets Cahill and Hagan	DATE 5-10-04				TIME 730pm	
WE ARE QUESTIONING YOU CONCERNING The murder by shooting of Abraham Cisse on 3-28-04 outside 7407 Andrews Ave.						
WARNINGS GIVEN BY	DATE				TIME	

ANSWERS

   (1)   (2)   (3)   (4)   (5)   (6)   (7)

Q1. Shaheed I am Det Cahill and this is Det Hagan and I interviewed you on 3-29-04 about this shooting and I would like to ask you some more questions about what you know about this incident is that OK?
A1. Yes. S H

Q2. Tell me in your own words what you know about the shooting of the pizza delivery man on 3-28-04 outside 7407 Andrews Ave?
A2. About 830pm I went outside my house and I saw Biggs standing outside my house and there was this other boy on a bicycle in front of the lawn of my neighbor's house at 7407 Andrews Ave. I asked BIGGS what he was doing there so late and he said "we had set something up" and then he asked if he could use my phone to call the pizza place to see if his order is ready. I then let him into my house and he made a phone call and he said on the phone "I want to check if my order is ready for 7407 Andrews Ave". Then he got off of the phone and he then went outside and I asked him what's up and he said they are on their way. Biggs then stood on the walkway of 7407 Andrews and I went back into the house. S H

Q3. Who did you see outside with Biggs when you were out there?
A3. The only other guy that I saw was the guy on the bike. S H

Q4. Can you describe the male on the bike to me?
A4. He was a b/m brown compl., 14-15 yrs old., about 130lbs and he was wearing all black skully pulled down to the top of his eyes. S H

Q5. Have you ever seen the boy on the bike before that night?
A5. No. S H

Q6. Did you observe anything else?
A6. After I went back into the house I went up to the 2nd floor front bedroom and I was looking out the window for about 10 minutes and that is when I saw the pizza guy pull up in his car and he parked his car in the middle of the street and he had his flashers on and I saw him get out of the car and he looked at Biggs and the guy on the bike and then he opened his back door and he took out the food and he walked around the back of the car and he went up the walkway of 7407 Andrews Ave and as the guy was walking up the walkway I saw Marty jog

RECORD [ ] YES [ ] NO	CHECKED BY: Shaheed Haith 5/10/04
REVIEWED BY:	

75-483

PAGE #2 OF

| INVESTIGATION INTERVIEW RECORD | CITY OF PHILADELPHIA |
| CONTINUATION SHEET | POLICE DEPARTMENT |

up behind the pizza guy and they both went out of my view. I then heard Marty's voice say "give me your fucking money" he said that about two or three times and then I heard a gunshot and I then got away from the window. I then went downstairs and I looked out my side window next to the door and I saw the pizza man laying on the step and he was bleeding from his head and he was gasping for air. I then went and called 911. S H

Q7. What is BIGGs full name?
A7. Keenan is his first name. I don't know his last name. S H

Q8. How long have you known Biggs?
A8. About three or four years. His grandmother lives on Penfield St. S H

Q9. What is Marty's full name?
A9. Martique Daughtry. S H

Q10. How long have you known Marty?
A10. About two years. S H

Q11. When you observed the man's body outside on your neighbor's step, did you see anybody around?
A11. No. S H

Q12. Why didn't you tell me this information when I first interviewed you on 3-28-04?
A12. I just didn't want to get involved. S H

Q13. Did you have anything to do with the planning or the robbery of the pizza delivery man?
A13. No. S H

Q14. Did you ever see Biggs or Marty with a gun before 3-28-04?
A14. Nope. S H

Q15. Did you observe anyone other than Biggs, Marty and the boy on the bike outside your house during this incident?
A15. No. S H

Q16. Is there anything else that you want to tell me about this incident?
A16. No. S H

Q17. Is everything that you have told me about this incident the truth?
A17. Yes. S H

Shaheed Haith 5/10/04

RECORD	CHECKED BY:
[ ] YES [ ] NO	
REVIEWED BY:	

75-483

Keenan Hudson

INVESTIGATION INTERVIEW RECORD				PHILADELPHIA POLICE DEPARTMENT HOMICIDE DIVISION		CASE # M04-81 INTERVIEWER: Det.John Cahill #919	
NAME Keenan HUDSON				AGE 15	RACE B	SEX M	DOB 1-16-89
ADDRESS 520 W. Rockland St.,Phila.19120				APARTMENT #		PHONE # 215-324-5888	
NAME OF EMPLOYMENT/SCHOOL							
ADDRESS OF EMPLOYMENT/SCHOOL				DEPARTMENT		PHONE #	
DATES OF PLANNED VACATIONS							
DATES OF PLANNED BUSINESS TRIPS							
NAME OF CLOSE RELATIVE Aunt: Brenda REGUSTERS							
ADDRESS same						PHONE# same	
PLACE OF INTERVIEW Homicide Rm 104 Police Hqts				DATE 5-28-04		TIME 1043am	
BROUGHT IN BY Det.Cahill				DATE 5-28-04		TIME 1030am	
WE ARE QUESTIONING YOU CONCERNING The murder by shooting of Abraham CISSE on 3-28-04 at 7407 Andrews Ave.							
WARNINGS GIVEN BY				DATE		TIME	
ANSWERS (1) (2) (3) (4) (5) (6) (7)							

Q. Keenan I am Det Cahill of the Homicide Division and also present in the room is your attorney Burton ROSE Esq and you have indicated to us that you wish to tell me what your involvement was in the murder by shooting of a pizza delivery on 3-28-04 at 7407 Andrews Ave is that correct?
A. Yes.

Q. Tell me in your own words what your involvement was?
A. I made the phone calls to the pizza place and my job was to bare hug the pizza man when he arrived. When the guy arrived he got out of his car and he looked at me and I pointed toward the house where Stephan was sitting on the step and the guy then walked up the path to the house pass me and then I went behind him and I put my arms around him from the back and as I grabbed the guy, Stephan took the food off of him. At this time Marty came up with the gun out and he was yelling things like, "give that shit up, give that shit up, and don't turn around" and as Marty was yelling this he held the gun to the guy's head. While this was going on I went into the guys right side pants pockets and I took out some change, about $3.00 dollars worth, and I then released the guy and Marty was still yelling at him and then I saw Marty shot the guy in the head. After Marty shot the guy Marty ran past me and we all met up at Justin's house.

Q. Who was involved in the planning of the robbery?
A. Me, Marty, Justin, Stephan, and Van.

Q. Who decided which pizza place to place the order with?
A. Marty found a menu inside his house and he told me to make the call and place the order.

Q. What did you order from the pizza place?
A. I ordered two pizzas, two or three cheese steaks, and thirty wings.

Q. How many times did you call the pizza place?
A. I called twice from Marty's house and once from Shaheed's house.

RECORD [ ] YES [ ] NO	CHECKED BY:
REVIEWED BY:	

75-483

PAGE #2 OF

| INVESTIGATION INTERVIEW RECORD | CITY OF PHILADELPHIA |
| *CONTINUATION SHEET* | POLICE DEPARTMENT |

Q. Who made the decision to rob the pizza man?
A. It was Marty and I said that I was in on the deal.

Q. What did you think was going to happen when the pizza man arrived?
A. I thought that we were going to beat him up and rob him and Justin was going to take the guys car.

Q. Did you know that Marty had a gun on him during the robbery?
A. Yes but I didn't know that he was going to use it.

Q. What did you think that Marty was going to do with the gun?
A. I didn't think that he was going to pull it out.

Q. When the robbery was being planned who was telling everyone what their job would be during the robbery?
A. It was Marty.

Q. What did Marty tell everyone to do?
A. He told me to bear hug the guy, he told Justin to take the car, he told Van to be a look out and he told Stephan to take the food, and Marty was going to hit the guy.

Q. Do you know what kind of gun that Marty used?
A. It was a .380.

Q. Do you know where Marty got the gun from?
A. He stole it from Kareem Lawson.

Q. What happened after the robbery/shooting when you got to Justin's house?
A. Marty was bragging that he shot the pizza guy and the rest of them were opening the food.

Q. Who was at Justin's house when you got there?
A. It was Justin, Marty and Stephan.

Q. Was Van at Justin's house?
A. No he was on his bike during the robbery and he probably went home.

Q. Did you give the pizza place a call back number when you placed the order?
A. Yes Marty gave me a number of somebody in his family to use as a call back number.

Q. What did you do with the money that you took from the pizza man?
A. I handed it to Marty and Stephan. Stephan said that he needed money to catch the bus.

Q. Did you ever see the pizza deliveryman before that night?
A. No.

Q. Did the pizza man resist in any way during the robbery?
A. No he just put his hands up.

Q. Did the pizza man have any type of weapon on him during the robbery?
A. No.

Q. How long did you stay at Justin's house after the robbery?
A. I was only there about fifteen seconds.

Q. What did you do after you left Justin's house?
A. I went to my Grand Mothers house at 1942 Penfield St.

RECORD	CHECKED BY:
[ ] YES [ ] NO	
REVIEWED BY:	

75-483

PAGE #3 OF

| INVESTIGATION INTERVIEW RECORD | CITY OF PHILADELPHIA |
| *CONTINUATION SHEET* | POLICE DEPARTMENT |

Q. Did Marty tell you what he did with the gun?
A. He told me that he gave it to somebody named Meeche and I believe that is Kareem Lawson.

Q. Do you know Kareem Daughtry?
A. Yes he is Marty's brother.

Q. Was Kareem Daughtry involved in the planning of or the execution of the robbery of the pizza man?
A. No.

Q. How long have you known Stephan?
A. About a week.

Q. Is there anything else that you want to tell me about this incident?
A. I'm real sorry about this incident. I didn't mean for anybody to get killed and from the bottom of my heart I am sorry for this.

RECORD	CHECKED BY:
[ ] YES [ ] NO	
REVIEWED BY:	

75-483

ENDORSEMENTS OF KEENAN HUDSON

THE HONORABLE BENJAMIN LERNER

When fifteen year old Keenan Hudson stood before me at his sentencing hearing, after pleading guilty to third degree murder, I knew that Pennsylvania law called for a substantial prison sentence. I implored Keenan not to let his crime and sentence define the rest of his life, but rather to seek out the people and prison programs which would enable him to succeed, rather than simply survive, when he returned to his community.

He has succeeded, and to a degree beyond all expectation. His book, "The Unspoken Truth and Life Story", is a brutally honest, day-by-day account of how he accomplished this. It should be read by everyone who wants to know more than popular slogans about crime, punishment and the possibility of real rehabilitation in our flawed prison system can teach them.

Judge Benjamin Lerner (RET)

REV. DR. SCOTT D. GRAUBARD

14 October, 2022

When one pictures a young man in the intercity with no stable family running the streets, they can predict the trajectory of the young man's life. His story might be as follows:

- The young man finds kindred spirits on the street
- The young man commits an offense and finds himself in the justice system
- The young man finds himself incarcerated. He learns the skills necessary to survive and thrive in prison.
- The young man is released from prison and returned to the streets. He uses the skills learned in prison to become a better criminal.

- The young man, who is not young anymore, reoffends and the cycle continues.

When one considers the typical story of a youthful offender it is easy to conclude that there is little possibility that they will change. There is little possibility that they CAN change. The recidivism rate within five years amongst juvenile offenders in the US is around 84%. People do not change.

But that is not the case with Keenan Hudson. Keenan defied the odds. He came to prison as a child. He sought to improve himself and never gave up on the dream of a different life outside of prison. Keenan accomplished if not the impossible, than the improbable. He changed.

Why was it possible for Keenan to change when so many others never do? Keenan Hudson met Jesus in prison. He surrendered his life to Him. He sought, even as an inmate, to live his life for God's Glory. And Jesus changed his life.

Keenan Hudson is the main actor in this incredible story. But this is a book about God. It describes how God's abundant grace love and mercy are the necessary ingredients for anyone to change. Without God change is impossible. Surrendered to God, change is inevitable.

Rev. Dr. Scott D. Graubard, DMin, BCC, ACBC Chaplain (retired)
SCI Albion, PA DOC

HILDERBRAND PELZER III

Keenan Hudson has written a timely and important book. For too long, we have missed the mark on realizing the impact of incarcerated youth and the valuable lessons they can share about social change and education in our communities. In *Keenan Hudson: The Unspoken Truth and Life Story*, Keenan Hudson provides much food for thought about the uplifting power of education. In this first-person narrative, you walk beside the author and learn from his life and insights and experience with the criminal justice system. This book is much more than an autobiography. Keenan Hudson shares how his incarceration and the people who helped him could motivate and inspire others. It is a must read for youths, parents, teachers, and community leaders at every level.

Hilderbrand Pelzer III, author of "Unlocking Potential: Organizing a School Inside a Prison"

MEET
KEENAN

After being certified as an adult at the age of fifteen and incarcerated for nearly fifteen years, Keenan Hudson has since transformed his life in positive ways and has used his experiences to motivate others, especially youth in engaging in activities to avoid becoming ensnared in the justice system. He took full advantage of educational services and self-development opportunities while incarcerated and persevered using lessons learned through education, religion, and music.

With this determination, he was able to establish several Businesses after settling into society. As a productive citizen, Keenan aims to share how his incarceration and the people who helped him could motivate and inspire those whom he encounters daily. This is particularly true for youth who may be struggling to overcome negative and adverse issues that Keenan is familiar with and where he can provide positive solutions through mentoring role modeling and teaching.

Stay Connected with Keenan's new books and programs at www.keenanhudson.com

CONNECT WITH KEENAN

Write to:

Keenan Hudson
521 Central Ave.
P.O. BOX   95
Cheltenham, PA 19012

Email: Keenanhudson215@gmail.com

Visit Website: www.keenanhudson.com

Social Media:

LinkedIn: Keenan Hudson

Facebook: Keenan Hudson

Instagram: Keenan_Hudson_215

Twitter: Keenan Hudson 9

Made in the USA
Las Vegas, NV
29 September 2023

78327417R00075